AMERICAN MOVIE PALACES

Rolf Achilles

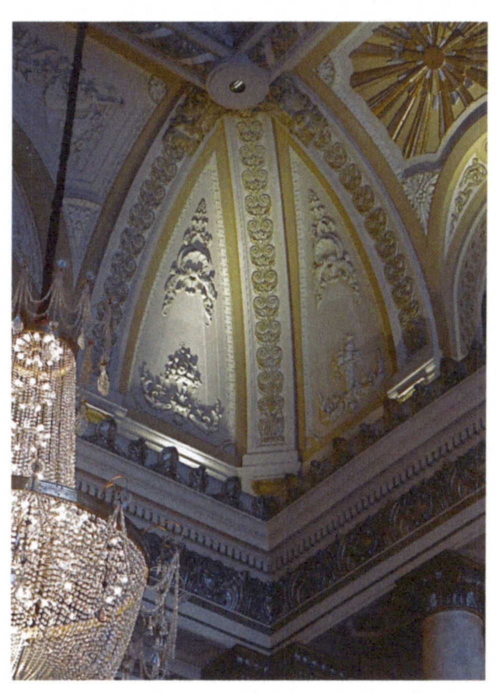

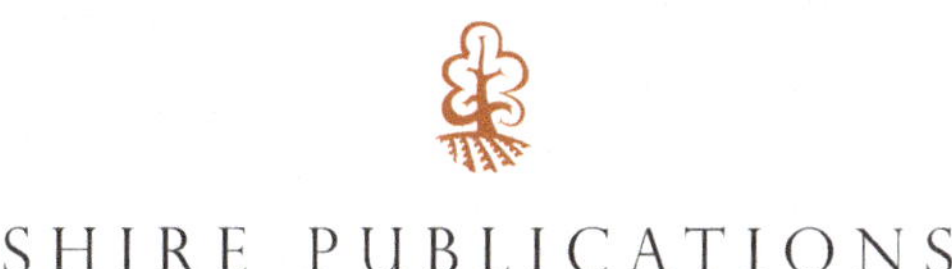

SHIRE PUBLICATIONS

Published by Shire Publications Ltd,
PO Box 883, Oxford, OX1 9PL, UK.
PO Box 3985, New York, NY 10185-3985, USA.
E-mail: shire@shirebooks.co.uk www.shirebooks.co.uk

First published 2013.
Transferred to digital print on demand 2016.

A CIP catalog record for this book is available from the British Library.

Shire Library no. 762. • ISBN-13: 978 0 74781 282 1

Rolf Achilles has asserted his right under the Copyright, Designs and Patents Act, 1988, to be identified as the author of this book.

Designed by Tony Truscott Designs, Sussex, UK
Typeset in Perpetua and Gill Sans.
Printed and bound in Great Britain.

COVER IMAGE

Opening Christmas Eve, 1928, with *Waterfront*, a First National film, and named for the founder of Richmond, Virginia, William Byrd II, the Byrd was built by architect/contractor Fred Bishop. Its interior is a mélange of Renaissance Revival designed by Arthur Brunet Studios. In keeping with the style of the day, its eleven magnificent chandeliers were fabricated of Bohemian crystal in Czechoslovakia. The Byrd was the first theatre in Virginia to be equipped with a sound system. It also has a Mighty Wurlitzer. In almost original condition, the Byrd continues to show 35mm films 365 days a year.
(Michael Kane Photography)

TITLE PAGE IMAGE

Rapp & Rapp's scagliola in the Chicago Theatre made faux look refined.

CONTENTS PAGE IMAGE

Elaborate plaster and velvet swags help find the Los Angeles Orpheum's grand stage.

PHOTOGRAPH ACKNOWLEDGEMENTS

Photographs are reproduced courtesy of: Flickr, page 6 (bottom); Tim Newark, page 62; Getty Images, page 4; Barbara Giesike, Badenweiler, Germany, page 11; Library of Congress, page 10; Christian Dionne, wikimedia commons, page 28; Corbis, page 49. All other images from the author's collection.

AUTHOR ACKNOWLEDGEMENTS

There are many more people involved in this book than I can thank here, but I would like to thank the Shire team, Tim Newark for suggesting this title and for letting me use one of his illustrations, Ruth Sheppard for her kind advice and editing, and Russell Butcher for being project manager. Thanks to the Theatre Historical Society of America for the fine work it and its membership is doing to keep the world informed on this uniquely American architectural form. Thanks also to Larry Lubliner and Tim Samuelson for conversations that helped me put movie palaces into context, to Debbie Dodge for her ongoing preservation commitment and for sharing her images of the interior of the Uptown Theatre in Chicago and to Alex Nerad for his preservation efforts and information on the Egyptian Theatre in De Kalb. Most of all, I'd like to thank Maral Hashemi for keeping this project going.

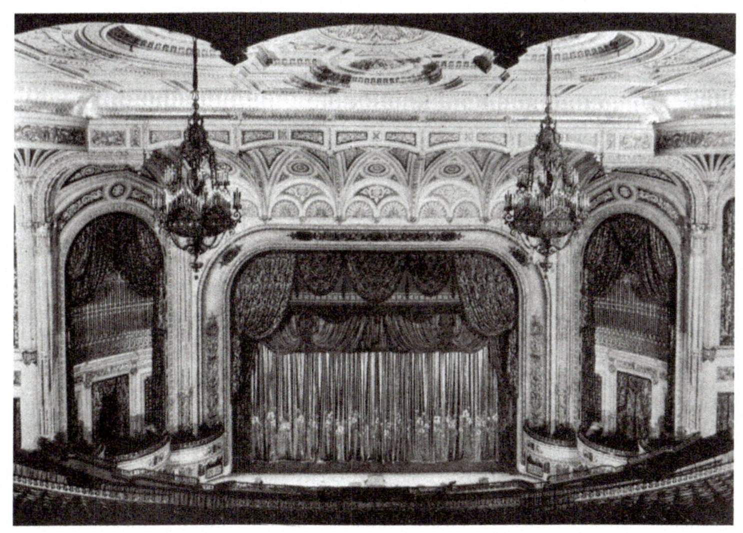

CONTENTS

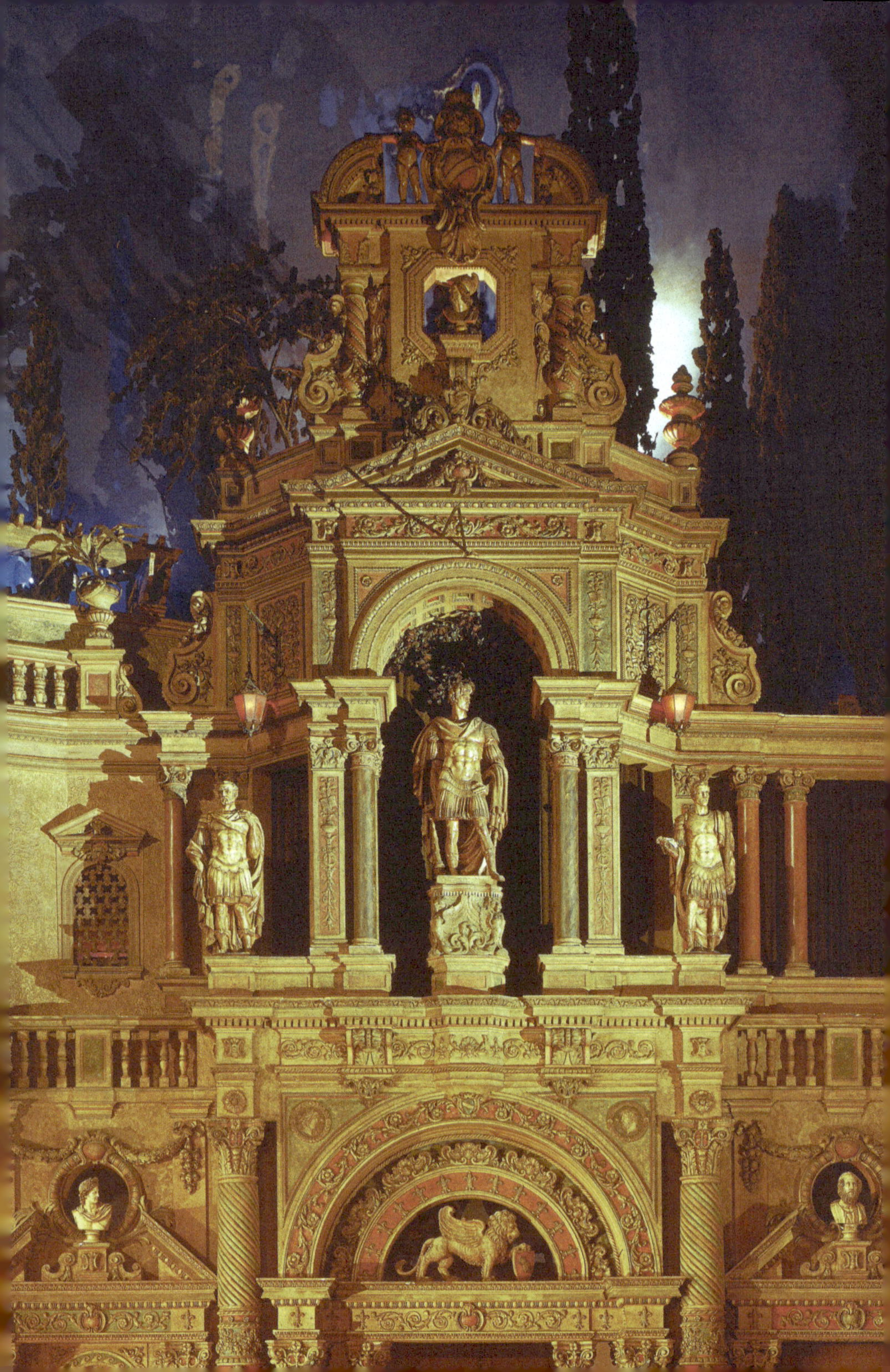

MOVIE PALACES

AS POP JEWELS TO COMMERCE, movie palaces were invented in America. They were born a Venus, rising beautiful and complete out of traditional theaters, yet unlike classical, rational buildings, their architects strove for their designs to embrace the new medium in specific traditional forms that resonated more emotionally than intellectually. Showing off with surface decoration that was extreme architecture, expressive, florid in its endless detailing, there was no depth, no deep meaning, no lessons to be sought on the outside of the building, on its walls. Inside, the ornamentation grew louder, more intense in its efforts to please eyes and stir emotions. An exotic world, unknown outside, was set by lighting—twinkling, moody or soothing—reflecting on silver or gold demons and gods, faux marble, lustrous stone, polished brass, and absorbed by thick red carpets: all to excite the eyes and stir the emotions.

The movie palace developed as quickly as the new medium it housed and legitimized in an exotic past of its own creation. Flickering like the films, styles and looks changed quickly. There was no shortage of beauty in the house or on the screen.

The story of movie palaces is also the story of the genius businessmen who made movies: creating life-like images out of light and selling dreams to the masses from which they themselves had emerged. It is about impresarios who made fortunes, traded them, and lost them. Mostly foreign-born, they had the American dream—they created the stars that glowed on screens and commissioned the architects and designers to reflect the new reality for the pleasure of the American public. Like the stuff of legends, theirs was a brief, yet glorious, existence.

MOVIES ENTERTAIN BETWEEN ACTS

In its infancy movies competed with penny arcades, enormous cycloramas, vaudeville theaters and the corner bar. For a time movies lived in recycled storefronts, squeezed into penny arcades and flickered between vaudeville performances on a full stage. Then, the visionary efforts of brothers

Opposite:
Like a film set, the plaster walls inside the Paradise Theatre in New York City evoke visions of Rome at its most fantastic.

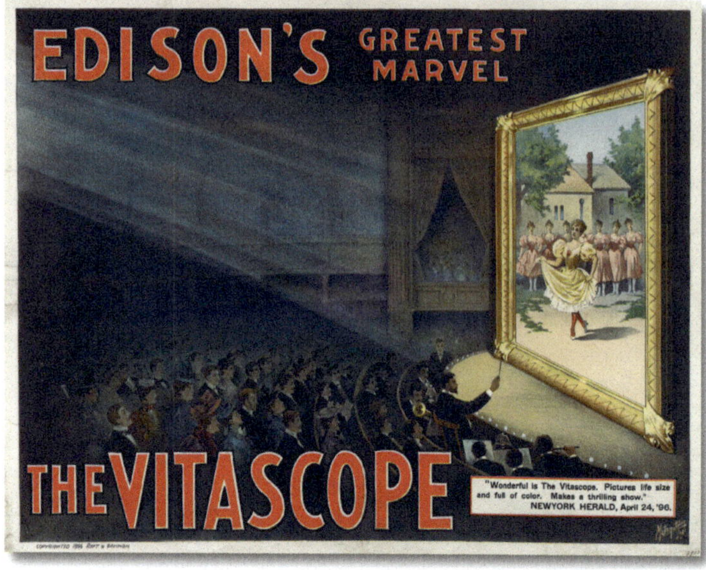

Edison's Vitascope was the first commercially successful motion picture projection machine. It made movie theatres possible.

Mitchel (also spelt Mitchell), Henry, and Moe Mark, supported by the technical expertise of Rudolph Wagner, resulted in the opening of Edison's Vitascope Theatre in the basement of the Ellicott Square Building in Buffalo, New York on October 19, 1896, with a film from France by Pathé Frères. According to the *Buffalo News*, admission was 3 cents and there were about seventy-five seats.

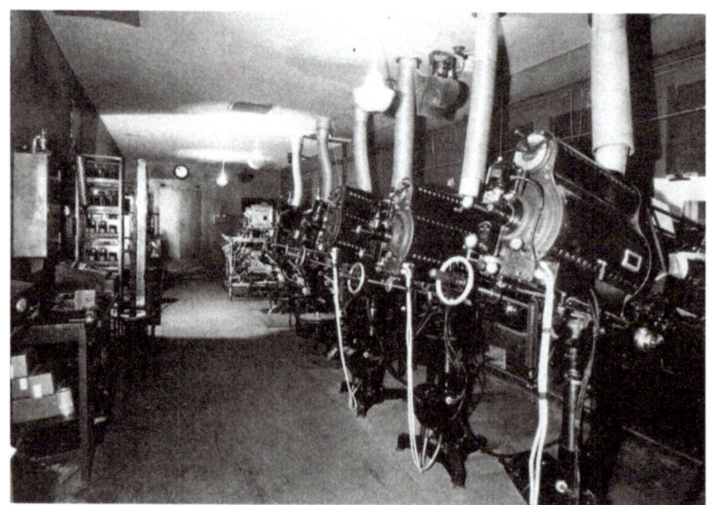

State-of-the-art projecting equipment in Loew's King Theatre, Brooklyn, NY, 1929. Rapp & Rapp were the architects, with interiors by Harold W. Rambush.

In June 1905, Harry Davis opened the first nickelodeon in Pittsburg, Pennsylvania, and quicker than a first kiss, the nickel-a-ticket moving pictures spread across the United States. Within two years, a hundred thousand Chicagoans per day visited a choice of 116 nickelodeons, eighteen 10-cent vaudeville houses and nineteen penny-arcades. The race was on.

Totally dependent on optics and machines, moving pictures replaced the traditional conventions of live performances with wholly new ones—gigantic in-your-face close-ups, the darkened room, text panels, emotionally charged music, and eventually, electrically enhanced sound, mesmerizing the audience and leaving them wanting more. The creators of movie pictures were urban and urbane, in it for the money as much as the art.

CLASSICAL: ADAMESQUE IS ELEGANT

The first movie palace in the United States was the Mark Strand Theatre, at 1579 Broadway (47th and Broadway) in New York City. Opened in 1914, by Mitchel and Moe Mark, the *New York Times* called it "… the most beautiful, comfortable and up-to-date theatre in the world." Mitchel Mark said he'd like to make "the Strand a 'National Institution' which would stand for all time as the model of moving picture palaces," and the *New York Times* drama critic Victor Watson wrote:

> It seemed like everyone in town had simultaneously arrived at the conclusion that a visit to the magnificent new movie playhouse was necessary. … If anyone had told me two years ago that the time would come when the finest-looking people in town would be going to the biggest newest theatre on Broadway for the purpose of seeing a motion picture I would have sent them down to visit … Bellevue Hospital.

In one night movies had become respectable and its first manager, Samuel "Roxy" Rothafel, had found his calling.

The Strand was designed by Thomas W. Lamb in what would be called his signature style, Adamesque—a neoclassicism brio that rose quietly out of a dash of Greek and Roman, a pinch of Italian Renaissance as marinated in pattern books of Scottish designer and architect Robert Adam (1728–92). Its 2,989 seats were soon filled with a crowd willing to pay a premium to sit through a movie and vaudeville acts in a hall replete with decorations that were in a style that was probably lost on many of them but that the Mark Brothers claimed to have cost one million dollars. Yet by 1929 The Strand's superlatives had started to fade, until they disappeared altogether. It closed on February 8, 1987, after which Mitchel Mark's "national institution which would stand for all time as a model"

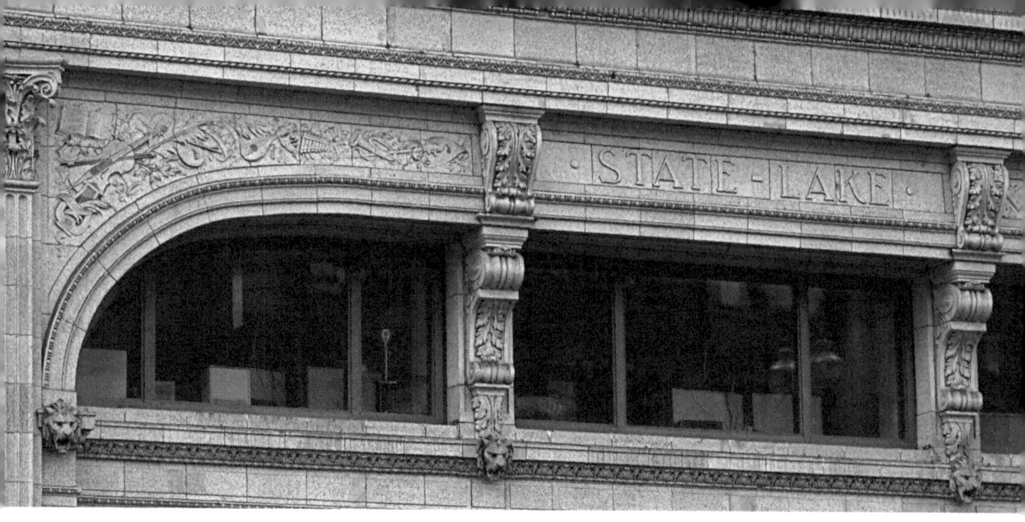

Rapp & Rapps' 1919 terracotta design for the State–Lake, the main Orpheum circuit theatre in Chicago, only hints at what's inside.

was demolished and replaced by the Morgan Stanley Building, a key to the redevelopment of family-friendly Times Square. Similar stories are heard across the nation.

The Strand's architect, Thomas White Lamb, was born in 1871 in Dundee, Scotland, and arrived in the United States in 1883. In 1942, his obituary claimed completion of some thirty theatres in high American style worldwide—Penang, Kolkata, Mumbai, Adelaide, Cairo, Durban, and Johannesburg.

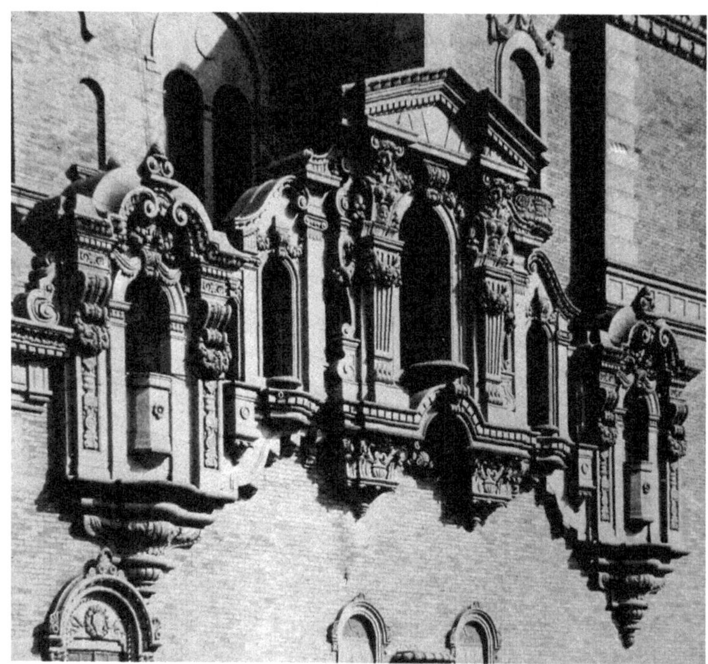

Faux balconies in bold, Renaissance-inspired terracotta, designed by Walter W. Ahlschlager, helped define the Roxy Theatre, New York.

Lamb's theatre façades could not be overlooked. By emphasizing large elements such as bands of polychrome terracotta with massive piers and muscular set-back windows, his façades set a pattern for how a theatre was to make visual noise to attract attention in a busy city. Lamb's façades were created mostly in terracotta and he worked with the leading companies of the day: Federal, South Amboy, Atlantic, and New York Architectural; in Chicago it was Northwest and American. Introduced in the 1850s by Andrew Jackson Downing, terracotta was a relative newcomer to American architecture. Because it was light and fireproof, terracotta became of great interest to the designers of movie palaces for façades, floors and ceilings. Possibly most important, terracotta was significantly less expensive than stone, it could be easily sculpted, molded quickly and mass-produced to exacting specifications. The convenience of terracotta was not lost on architects designing theatres throughout the country.

Theatres seem to have become Lamb's specialty; by 1912 he had completed thirty in New York City alone. He went on to build theatres for William Fox—such as the Audubon at 165th Street and Broadway—and his RKO on 81st Street at Broadway still retains some of its original terracotta and two-story Roman arcade, though today it cloaks a Staples store.

When Thomas W. Lamb's Regent Theatre opened in February 1913 with John Bunny in *Pandora's Box*, at 1912 Seventh Avenue, New York City in what was then a German-American part of Harlem, the Regent was hailed as an "all picture house." From the street it looked Doge Palace Venetian; inside it was Spanish-Moorish inspired with thick deep blue and gold carpet and satin-paneled walls leading up to a grand ceiling mural, *La Rendición de Granada* (*The Surrender of Granada*) envisioned after a painting of the same name by Francisco Pradilla (1848–1921).

Renaissance– and Adamesque–inspired theatres are not just found in large cities. Savannah, Georgia is home to the Lucas Theatre, designed by theatre architect C. K. Howell and built in 1921 by Arthur Lucas, an owner of more than twenty theatres in the south, but the Lucas in Savannah is the only one to carry his name. The very fine interior sculpture and detailing is probably the work of Richmond, Virginia-based Italian-trained sculptor Ferruccio Legnaioli.

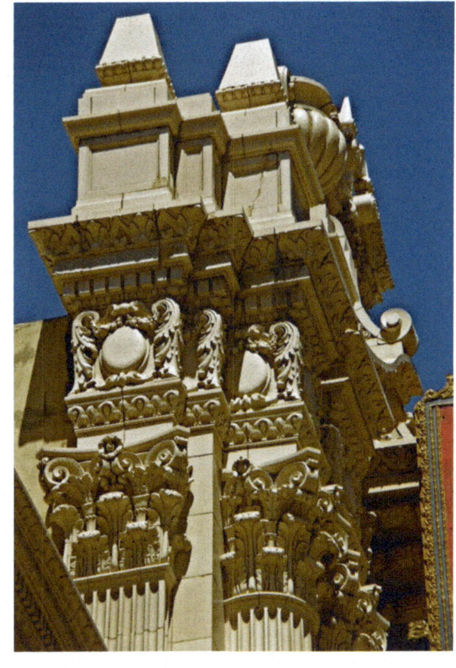

The bravura of a movie set fabricated in terracotta defines the façade of the Los Angeles Theatre.

MEN CREATE MOVIES

Another early seer of the power of films was Adolph Zukor. He was born in 1873 as Adolph Cukor into a Jewish family in the thriving shtetl of Ricse, eastern Hungary, at the time Austria-Hungary. He would die at the age of 103 in Los Angeles in 1976. Zukor arrived in the United States at the age of sixteen and settled in New York City, first working in an upholstery shop, then becoming apprenticed to a furrier. By 1895 he was in Chicago running his own store, Zukor's Novelty Fur Company, with twenty-five employees. Back in New York by 1903, he had a sumptuous apartment in a Jewish neighborhood at 111th Street and Seventh Avenue.

That same year, his cousin, Max Goldstein, approached him for a loan so that he could invest in Mitchel Mark's new Automatic Vaudeville Company on 14th Street in New York City which was going to feature Thomas Edison's three new marvels—phonographs, electric lights and moving pictures—in one room. Zukor made the loan, but also offered his cousin a partnership in an identical business, with a third partner, Marcus Loew. Loew (1870–1972), born into a very poor Jewish family in New York City, was turning his meager savings into pioneering the film industry and soon, with two other partners, Joseph Schenck and Nicholas Schenck, Zukor and Goldstein helped Loew founded Loew's Theatres. By 1903/4, Marcus Loew had intuitively sensed the potential of the early film industry and soon managed and owned several theatres in New York City, Boston and Philadelphia. With trusted partners and an understanding of this new urban business, he went national, then international. In 1920 he purchased Metro Pictures, then acquired Goldwyn Picture Corp, from Samuel Goldwyn in Culver City, California, who owned the "Leo the Lion" trademark. After much careful negotiation Loew also got Louis B. Mayer to join his group. Lucky for Loew, Mayer brought along Irving Thalberg, his genius chief of production. Loew's group eventually became Metro-Goldwyn-Mayer—known around the world for its roaring lion logo and its acronym, MGM. Though Loew was in the movies, by the 1920s he saw it as a business to own and manage, and did not get involved in the production of movies unlike most of his contemporaries.

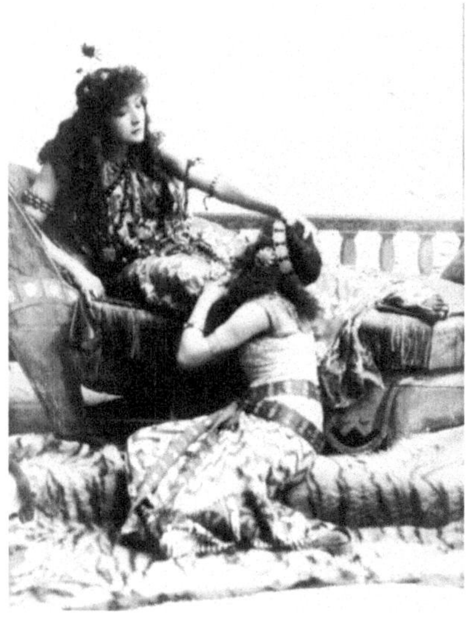

Sarah Bernhardt, photo by Napoleon Sarony, c. 1891, in a composition that looks much like an early film set.

When he started in the movie business, Adolph Zukor, an immigrant, may have seen something personal in them, too. Immigrants were a primary audience of the movies, and often learning English from the movies. After all, a film's word panels had to be read to know what the lips were mouthing and the eyes were implying. For Zukor it may have been a way to teach his fellow immigrants a new language while introducing them to a new culture, and all for the one low price of admission to the movies. The popcorn came later.

In 1912, Zukor laid out $18,000 to establish Famous Players Film Company and to become the exclusive American distributor for the French film, *Les Amours de la reine Elisabeth* (*The Loves of Queen Elizabeth*) starring Sarah Bernhardt. His advertising banner read, "Famous Players in Famous Plays." At the time, there was no one more famous in the world than Sarah Bernhardt.

A year later, Zukor had produced an adventure film based on the 1894 novel by Anthony Hope—*The Prisoner of Zenda*—and purchased an armory on 26th Street in New York City, converting it into Chelsea Studios. He soon formed a partnership with co-producer Jesse L. Lasky. In 1919, the company became Famous Players-Lasky, which eventually morphed into Paramount Pictures. Along the way Zukor's studio became the first to vertically integrate production, distribution and exhibition. Others in the movie industry were also involved—some led, more followed. By 1930, Warner Bros., Loew's, Fox and RKO had followed Lasky's lead, and they became known as the "Big Five." The vertical integration of the "Big Five" controlled the film industry. Then came the Depression. Between 1930 and 1932, the number of people going to the movies each week dropped by a third—from ninety million to sixty million. This quickly affected the studios' bottom line. Fox was in trouble first. By 1935, after merging with a small independent filmmaker, Fox became known as Twentieth Century-Fox. Loew's was by this time part of Fox and went into receivership, then into a trust emerging as a public stock company with the name MGM. Paramount went into receivership in 1933, followed by bankruptcy and emerged reorganized in 1936. In 1934 RKO faced bankruptcy, and took five years to reorganize. Universal sold all its theatres, and still went into receivership in 1933, before being reorganized in 1936. Warner, Columbia and United Artists survived intact.

Starved by its business model, government intervention and audiences with less spending money, the movies as a business began a slow decline. This decline is reflected in the architecture of movie palaces too. As the glorious architectural fantasies of the 1920s and early 1930s blossomed across the nation, they began to be challenged by the more severe and rationally streamlined modern theatres. Their reaction was like ill-equipped soldiers in glorious uniforms: they fell. In turn, streamlined theatres too were ill-equipped to meet the changes in America's media cravings of the 1950s and 1960s. By the 1970s, the public's interest in movie palaces had all but disappeared, resulting in the palaces and the once-aggressive moderns being shuttered, neglected, and demolished.

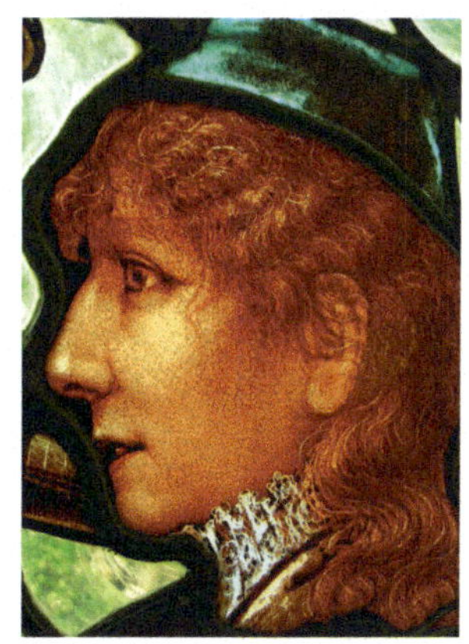

The first truly international star of the stage, Sarah Bernhardt, here in a stained glass window portrait, c. 1900, was also popular on the screen.

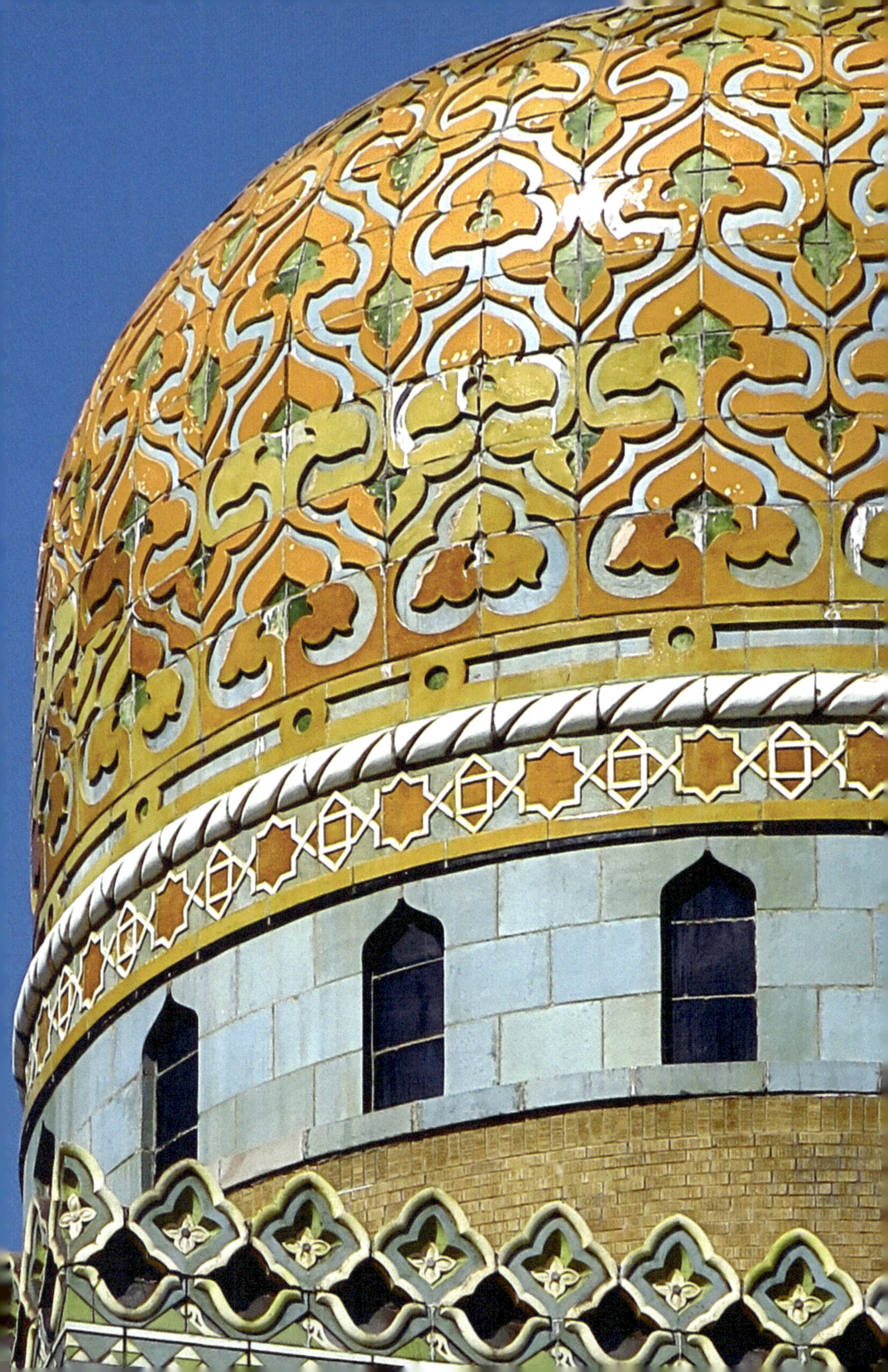

MOVIE PALACES STAND OUT

POPULARITY AND MONEY had come quickly to the movies. In 1922 about 40 percent of all Americans went to the movies each week. By 1930, this had risen to over 90 percent. Each week tens of millions of Americans sat in the dark for hours eating popcorn, drinking Coca-Cola and falling in love over and over again with their favorite stars. By the mid-1920s several different film-showing functions had crystallized and along with them the audience's expectations of what the theatre should look like: first runs were opulent, often ostentatious, palaces. Neighborhood theatres were almost always second run, and more modest, depending on their location. Third- and fourth-run theatres were usually very local and modest. Each generation of a film's appearance had its own building type, venue and audience.

In 1908, the Nasser Brothers—William, Elias and George—started a nickelodeon in the Castro neighborhood of San Francisco. Two years later the brothers opened the original Castro Theatre and a dozen years later opened the current 1,407-seat Castro, at 429 Castro Street. Designed by Timothy L. Pflueger in 1922, with its Mexican Colonial Baroque façade an example of a nascent national trend, the Castro's scrollwork and plaques are a homage by Pflueger to the nearby basilica of Mission Dolores. Using a direct model as inspiration, Pflueger's Castro is an early example of the influence of Mexican and Spanish Baroque on movie palaces. This style became very popular across the United States in the later 1920s until it was replaced by the sleek lines of Modernism in the early 1930s, when the streamlined look was popularized by the highly acclaimed Century of Progress Exhibition of 1933–34 in Chicago.

The Castro's street entrance, with a red and gray grid tile floor and floral tile-glazed gazebo box office and a wall of wooden doors framed in Spanish/Portuguese-inspired tiles, is all original from 1922. The interior is not specifically Spanish Baroque, but is instead a fantasy mix of Mediterranean and oriental inspirations. The Baroque's alternating concave and convex walls are covered with linear scraffito murals carved directly into the wet plaster, a technique rarely found in American movie palaces. The Art

Opposite: The tiles on the dome of the New Regal look like they belong in Isfahan more than along 79th Street in Chicago.

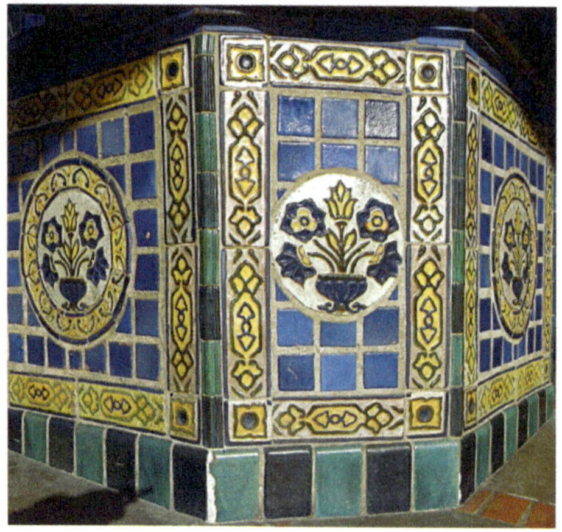

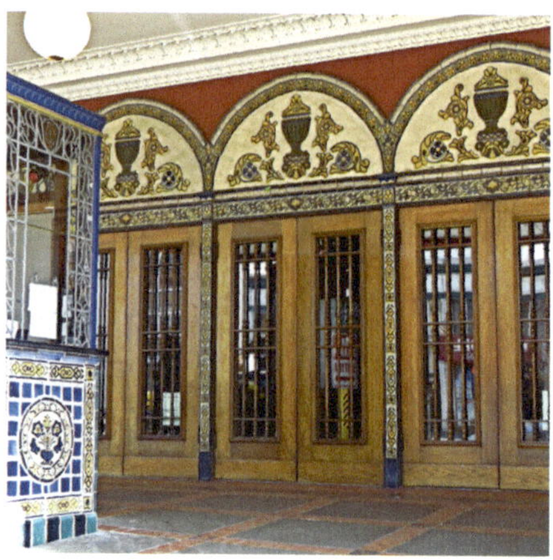

Tiles were a popular box office surround in the 1920s, even if they did not directly relate to the overall theme of the architecture. Castro Theatre, San Francisco (1922).

Above right: Modestly Spanish Baroque-inspired tiles and plaster molding greet the box office crowds entering the Castro Theatre, San Francisco.

Deco chandelier dates from 1937, when a fire destroyed the original parchment one. At about the same time the marquee and the vertical neon sign were added to the façade.

Two stairs lead from the lobby to the mezzanine and balcony, each with a grand Baroque-inspired newel post. Large gold frames flank their walls. A "Mighty Wurlitzer" organ replaced the original Conn organ in 1982. The film *Milk*—about the first openly gay person to be elected to public office in California as a member of the San Francisco Board of Supervisors (Sean Penn

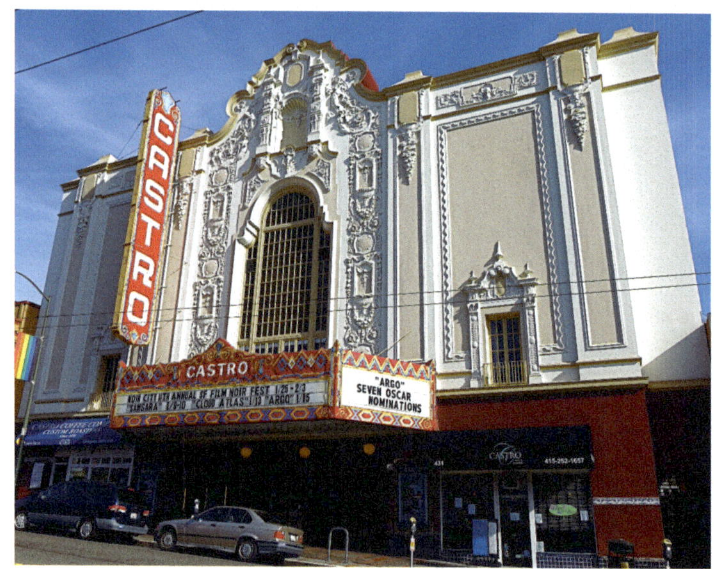

A nearby church façade is said to have inspired Timothy Pflueger's façade for the neighborhood Castro Theatre in San Francisco.

won an Academy Award in the title role)—had its world premier at the Castro in November 2008.

THEATRES HAVE STYLE

Timothy Ludwig Pflueger was born in 1892 in San Francisco to German immigrants living on Potrero Hill. He died in 1946, a highly respected and acclaimed San Francisco architect and interior designer. Starting as a draftsman and quickly gaining a reputation for working in various styles—Beaux-Arts, Mission Revival, Neoclassical, neo-Mayan—individually or all in one project, Pflueger designed a wide range of buildings and interiors. After completing the Castro for the Nasser brothers, Pflueger would complete another neighborhood theatre, the Alhambra in 1926, in a Moorish Revival style. Pflueger went on to build three more theatres in central Californian cities: the Tular Theatre in Tular (1927), which featured motifs

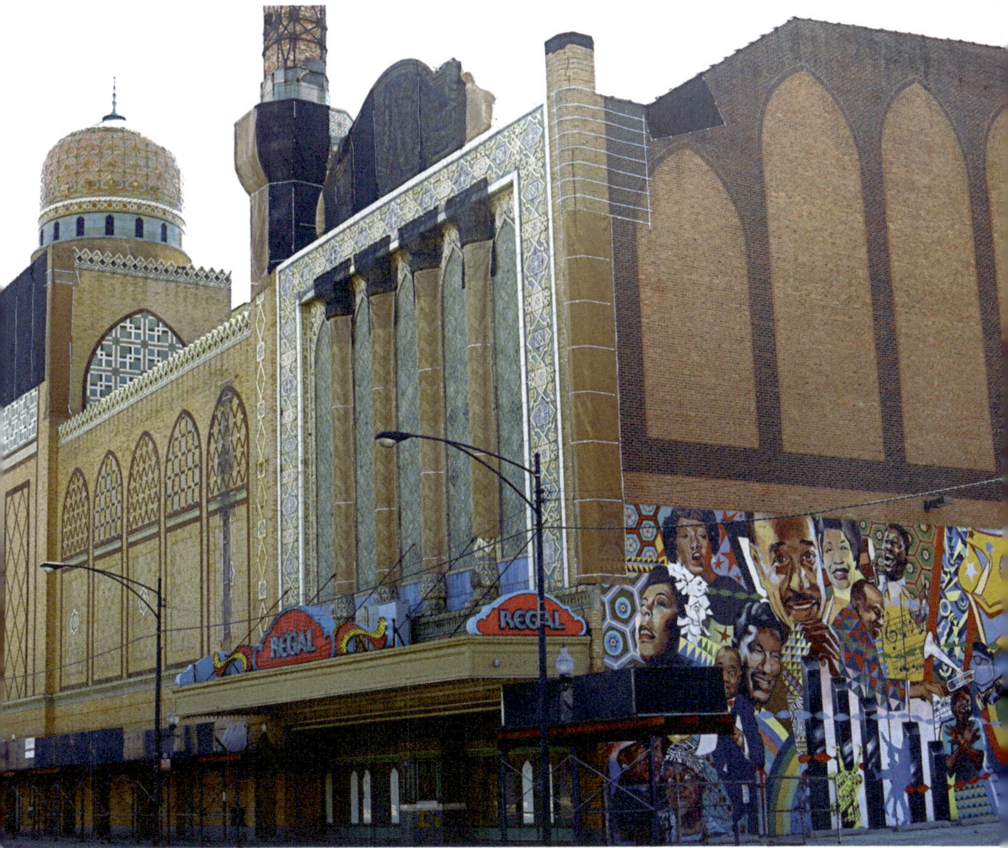

Chicago's New Regal Theatre was once called the Alhambra.

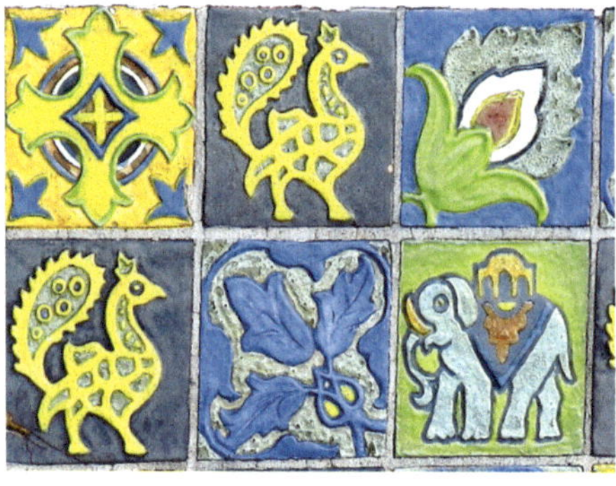

Right: The New Regal's tiles look Persian, but may have been designed and fabricated in Chicago.

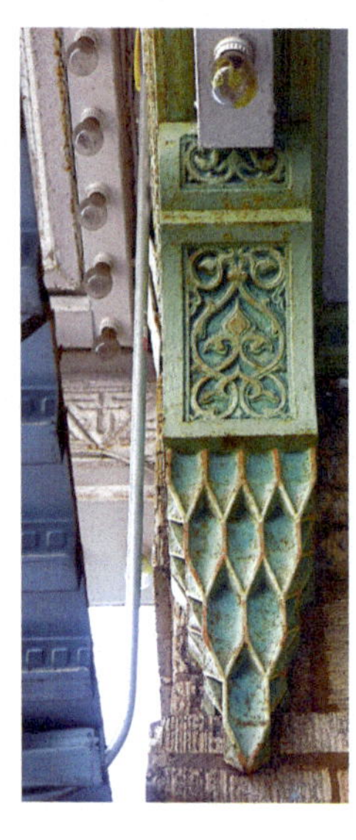

Far right: Even a cast-iron corbel looks decidedly Islamic. No detail was neglected at Chicago's New Regal.

based on the Ishtar Gate; the Senator Theatre in Chico (1928), which was eclectic in its Egyptian, Moorish, Asian and Aztec detailing; and the State Theatre in Oroville in Spanish Colonial, which was completed in 1928. The grand Paramount Oakland followed in 1929.

Looking up at the tower of John Eberson's New Regal Theatre at 1641 East 79th Street, in Chicago, you can almost hear a muezzin calling the devout to prayer. Originally opening as the Avalon Theatre on August 29, 1927, for the Cooney Brothers circuit, the "Moorish"-inspired New Regal is striking, with its exterior reminiscent of a great Persian mosque, and the Central Asian-decorated interior seating over 2,500. Hanging from the lobby ceiling is a "flying" oriental carpet. Lower on the lobby walls are mosaic murals. Winged lions, perhaps Persian Shedu, or perhaps the Lion of Venice, representing the Evangelist St. Mark, guard the stage.

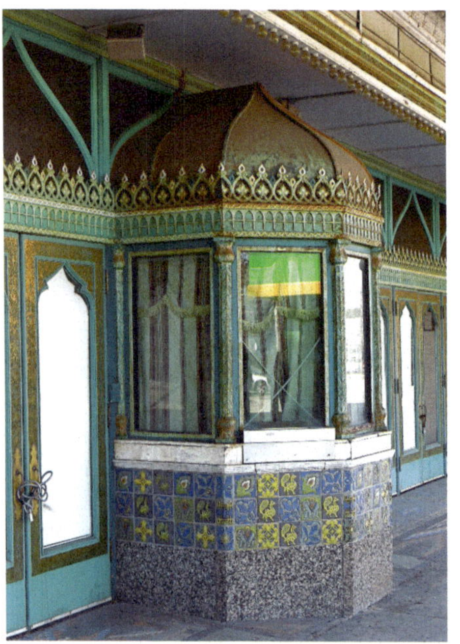

Colorful tiles enhance the box office of the New Regal in Chicago.

MOVIE PALACES ARE FOR EVERYONE

The first sighting of a new feature production film would take place in a palace specifically designed to enhance the projected fantasies dreamed up by architects employed by the film studios. Large cities, such as New York, Chicago, Los Angeles or Detroit, had several elegant and centrally located movie palaces. Smaller cities or neighborhoods in a large city had one, sometimes two or even three theatres, located on a thriving commercial street or on a side street just off the hub showing films several weeks after their premiers.

EGYPTOMANIA

The architects of small-town theatres often had aspirations to emulate, sometimes even capture, the spirit of the big city palaces seen in the

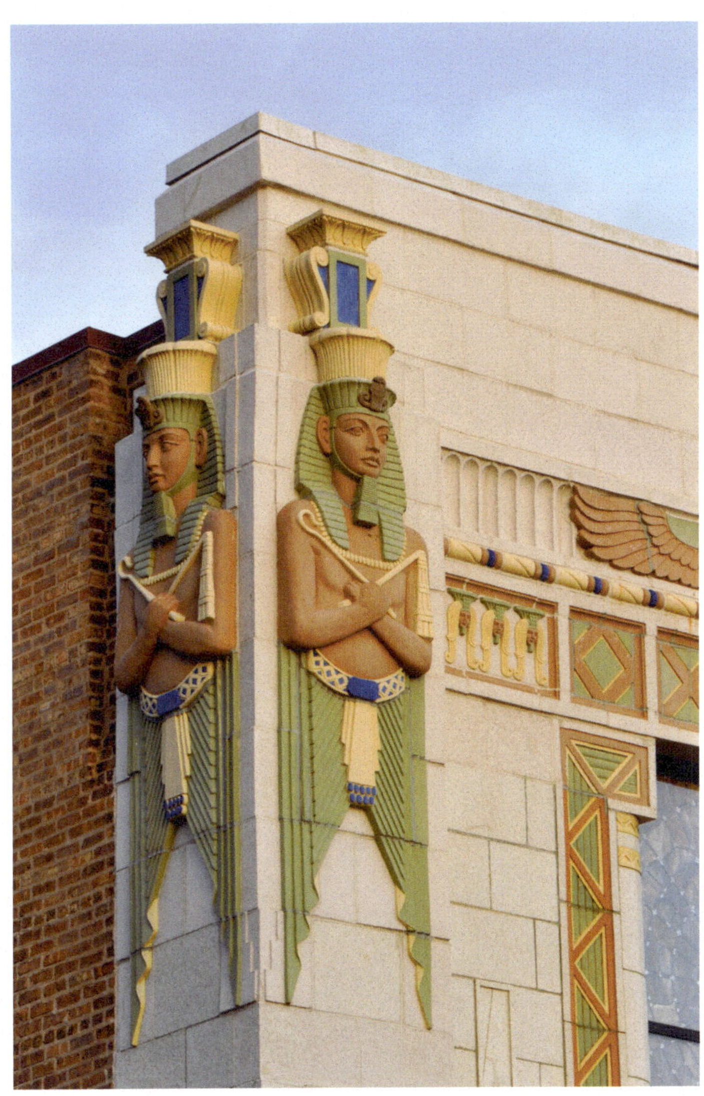

King Tutankhamun was all the rage, but Elmer F. Behrns, architect of the Egyptian Theatre in DeKalb and amateur Egyptologist, chose Ramses II.

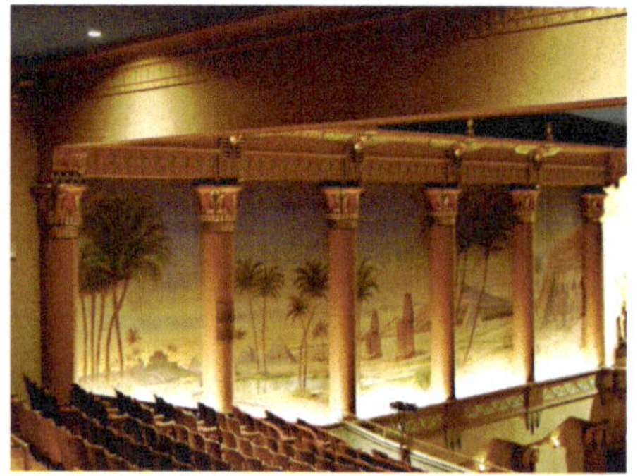

newsreels, only on a more modest scale and to a more modest budget. A fine example of a small city's fanciful theatre is the Egyptian, which opened in December 1929 at 135 N. 2nd Street, DeKalb, Illinois. The architect was Elmer F. Behrns, who fancied himself an amateur Egyptologist. Inspired by the national fascination with all things ancient Egyptian after Howard Carter's discovery of the tomb of King Tutankhamun in 1922 and the exotic success of Grauman's Egyptian Theatre in Hollywood,

Every surface in DeKalb's Egyptian Theatre is themed, as shown by these murals in the interior.

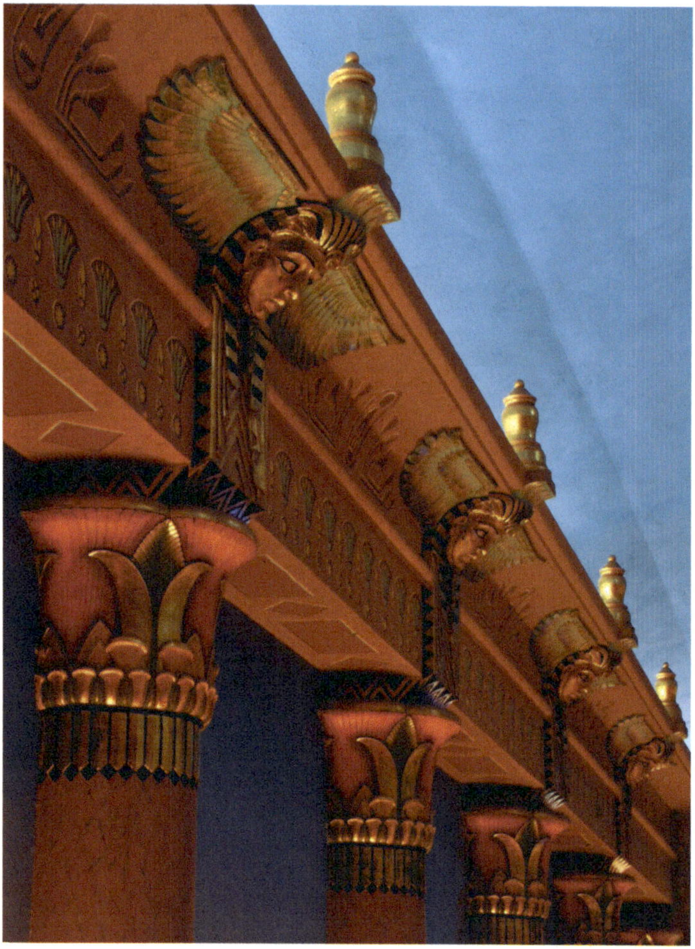

Egyptomania made fine ornamentation in DeKalb's Egyptian Theatre in 1929.

Behrns's Egyptian has a more elegant take on ancient Egypt than any of the several other Egyptian-inspired theatres in the United States. Fine exterior polychrome terracotta busts (probably by the American Terra Cotta Company, Terra Cotta, in Crystal Lake, Illinois) resemble Ramses II in powerful bodybuilding pose, and a large window over the entrance shows a scarab holding the sun god Ra. Inside, the patrons are watched over by winged heads of pharaohs interspersed with bunches of lotus. Two large murals, depicting pyramids and desert, add more exotica to the auditorium.

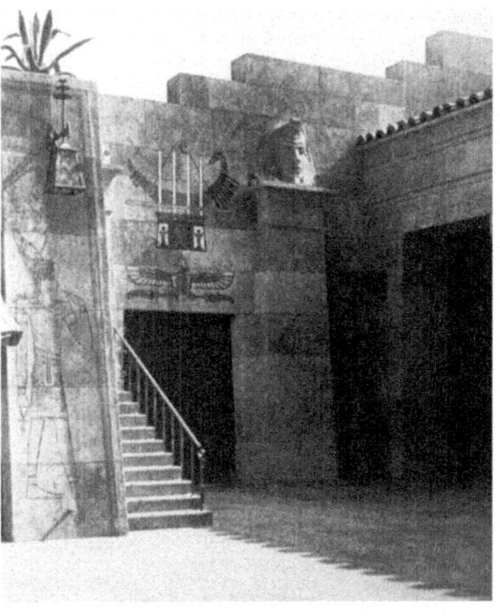

References to Ramses II abound in Hollywood's Egyptian Theatre.

In comparison, the Egyptian in Hollywood is austere. Standing at 6706–6712 Hollywood Boulevard, it was designed by Los Angeles-based Meyer & Holler (Gabriel S. Meyer, 1874–1955 & Philip W. Holler, 1869–1942) and constructed by the Milwaukee Building Company for showman Sid Grauman and real estate developer Charles E. Toberman. Probably the world's most famous Egyptomania movie palace, it opened on October 18, 1922, two weeks after Howard Carter announced his discovery

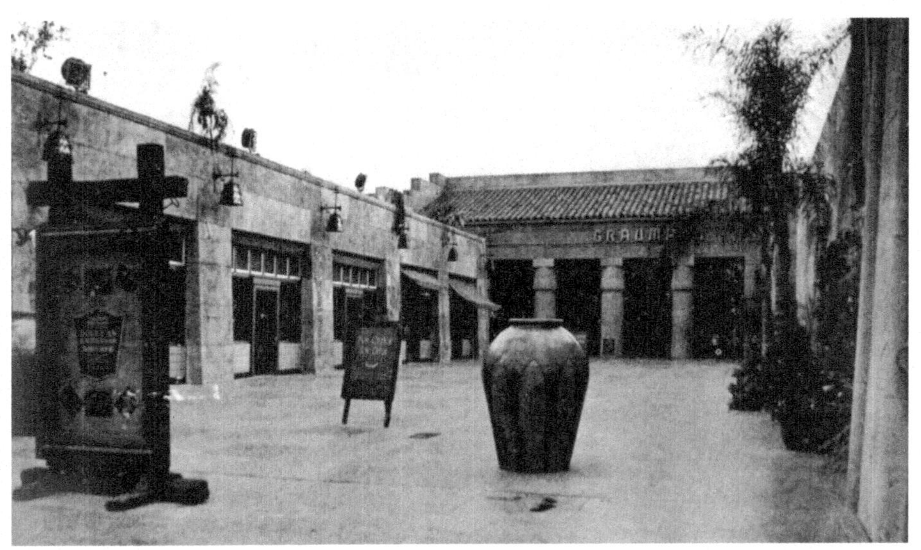

The great courtyard of the Hollywood Egyptian Theatre (1922), by Meyer & Holler, expresses Egyptian grandeur.

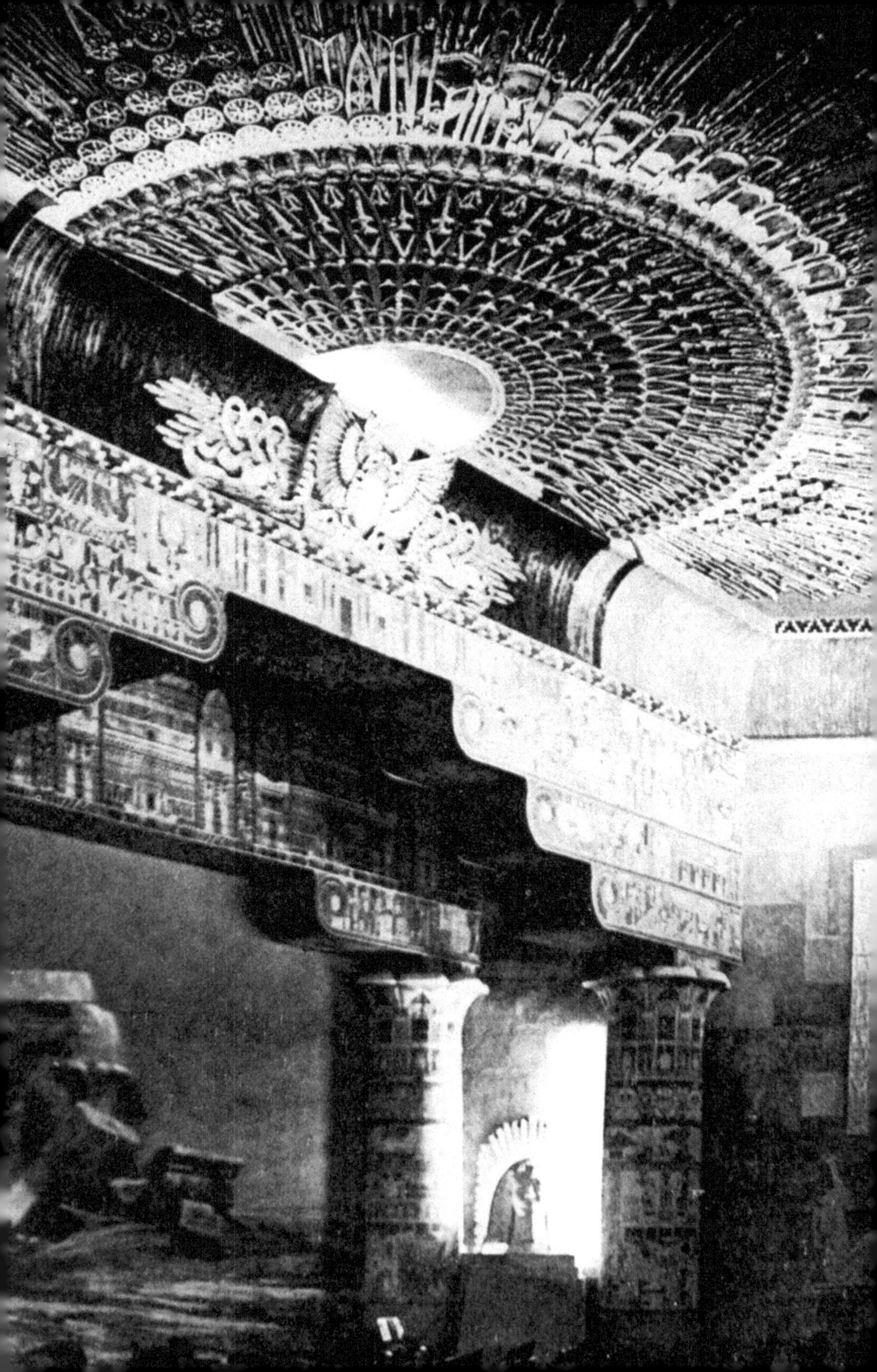

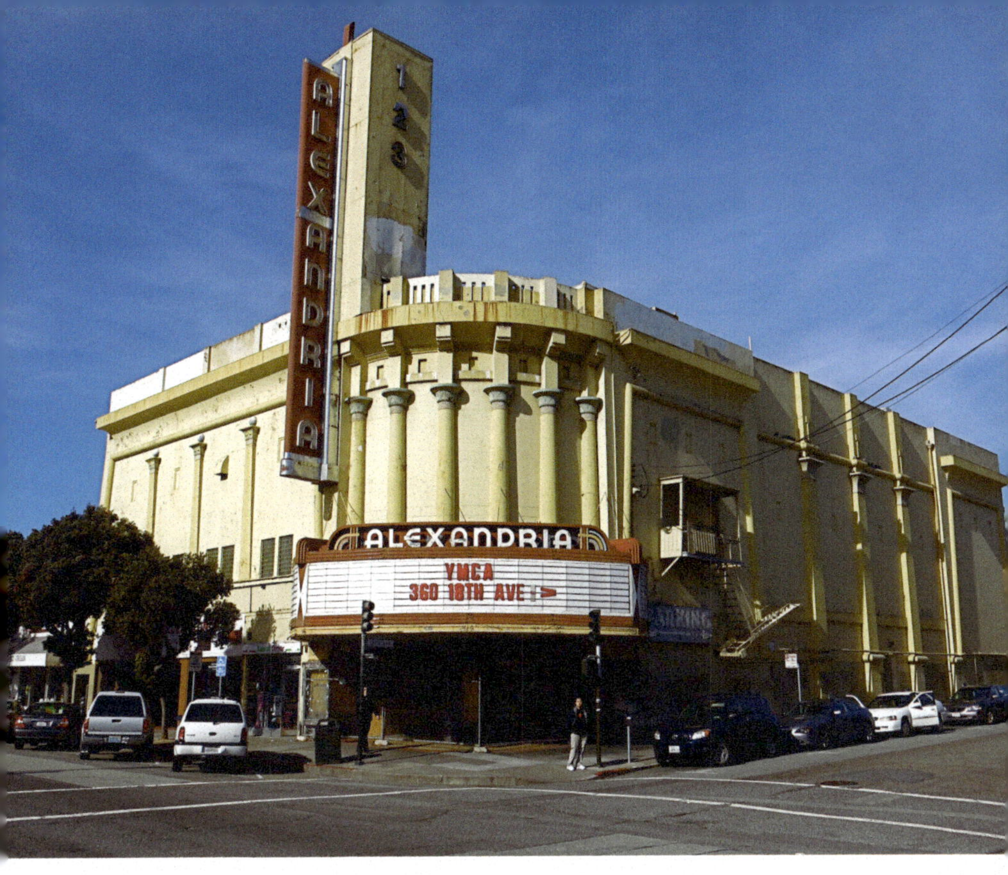

A bit of neighborly Egyptomania, the Alexandria Theatre in San Francisco.

of the tomb of King Tutankhamun. It opened to international acclaim as the first-ever venue for a Hollywood premier—*Robin Hood* starring Douglas Fairbanks. The entrance hall is a courtyard, designed to host red-carpet premiers. Open to the sky, it is 150 feet long and 45 feet wide, lined with accurate Egyptian-styled paintings and hieroglyphs and complete with fountain and palms. Inside the Egyptian theme continues, lavishly. Hollywood's Egyptian is an inspired follower of a long tradition of Egyptomania, popularized in the late eighteenth and early nineteenth centuries in England and Germany by stories and dreams and then furthered by Napoleon's interest in Egyptian art, such as obelisks and the Rosetta stone. Several Egyptomania-themed theatres survive.

The Alexandria in San Francisco's Richmond district, 5400 Geary Boulevard, opened November 26, 1923 as a leading second-run theatre. Designed by Reid Brothers for Oppenheimer & Levin, it was a grand neighborhood Egyptomania theatre in its day. It is rumored that beneath its remodeling, the original atmospheric ceiling with its twinkling lights survives and that in the lobby, lotus columns and colorful glyphs still wait to be uncovered from beneath layers of paint.

Opposite: Decorated by Sid Grauman, the interior of Hollywood's Egyptian looked more like a giant Egyptian tomb than seating for a movie. Despite the poor quality of this picture, it is a valuable record – the heiroglyph panels and pillars below the scarab beetle in the freeze were lost in refurbishment.

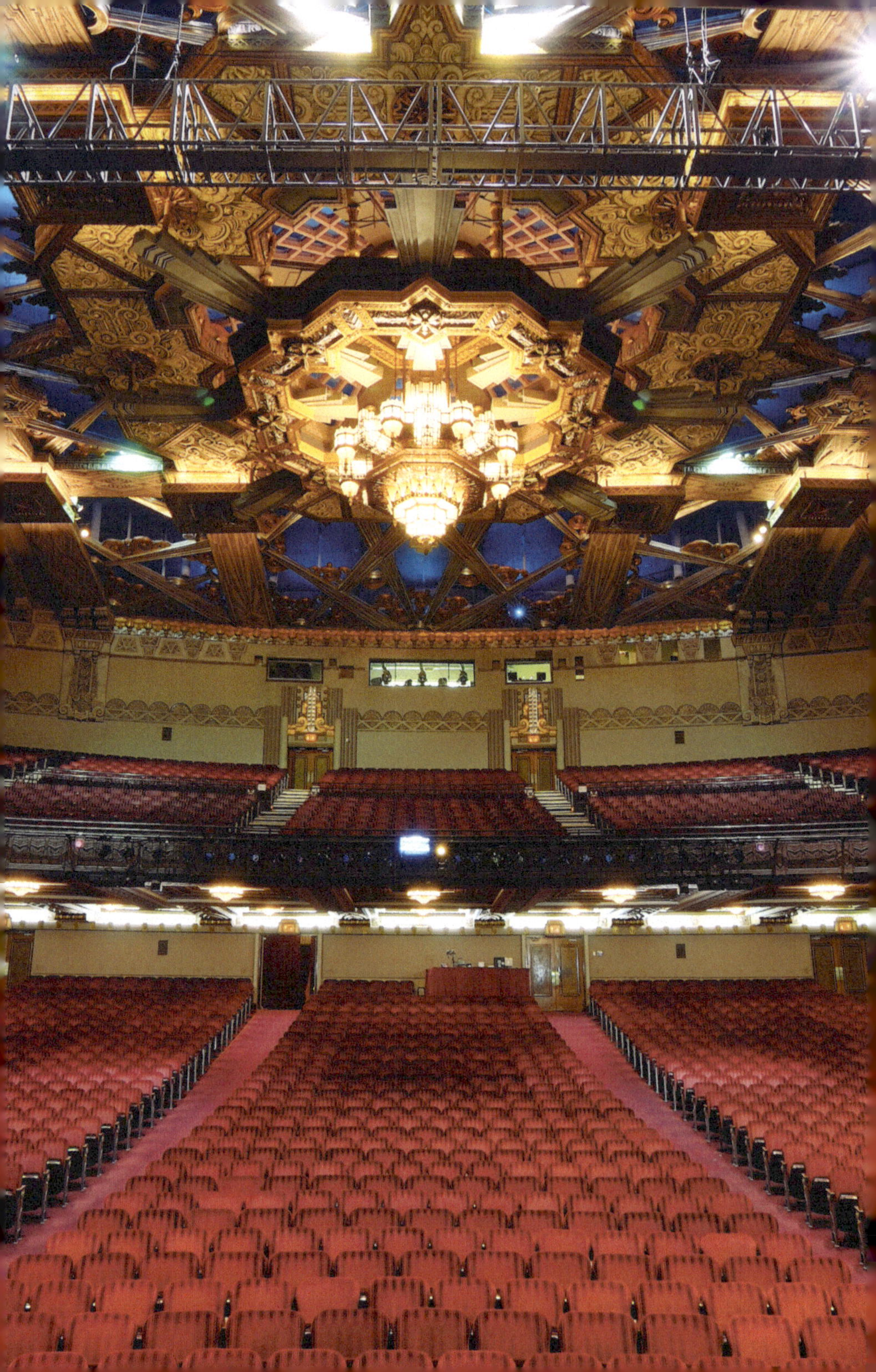

THERAPEUTIC FANTASY INSIDE A MOVIE PALACE

BY THE LATE 1920s, movie palaces were either "hard top" or "atmospheric," two distinct styles, each dreamy, and each common throughout the United States. The "hard top" retained the traditions of live theatre, with its roots in the classical Greek odeon. The exotica exuded by these theatres made them very popular for a decade, but soon the dust kitties of time gathered in every picturesque crack and corner until the hard edge of 1930s streamlined Modernism took over their conventional dreams.

The other type was the atmospheric theatre with its false plaster ceiling painted as a deep-blue night sky and pierced to reveal twinkling lights. Invented by John Eberson, the first fully atmospheric theatre was the Houston Majestic (1923) where the audience sat as if in a village piazza beneath the night sky. Even before the movie started, Eberson intended the house to serve up a "therapeutic fantasy, soothing the nerves and calming perturbing thoughts," in a mystical darkness achieved with little more than a ceiling painted blue and punctured with small holes through which low-wattage bulbs appeared to "twinkle." For an extra treat, some theatres projected slowly moving clouds across their night sky by way of the Brenograph, a machine that combined spotlight, slide projection and moving effects.

John Eberson was born in 1875 in Cernauti, Bukovina, a region of Romania in Austria-Hungary, and had studied electrical engineering in Vienna before he settled in St. Louis in 1901. Eberson's most famous movie palace was the Paradise Theatre in Chicago, opened in 1928, by Balaban and Katz. By the late 1920s there were at least two or three copies for every one of the some five hundred theatres John Eberson had designed, both in the United States and elsewhere. Their proliferation was aided by their cost efficiency, making them an easy choice for both developer and impresario, yet only about eighteen of Eberson's atmospheric theatres survive. Opening in 1928, the Palace Theatre in Marion, Ohio, is a Moorish courtyard seating 1,548. Besides being a surviving atmospheric, its Moorish alcoves house the unique attraction of a collection of taxidermied birds, including John Eberson's own late parrot. Eberson himself died in 1964, almost forgotten.

Opposite: The auditorium of Hollywood's Pantages in 2013.

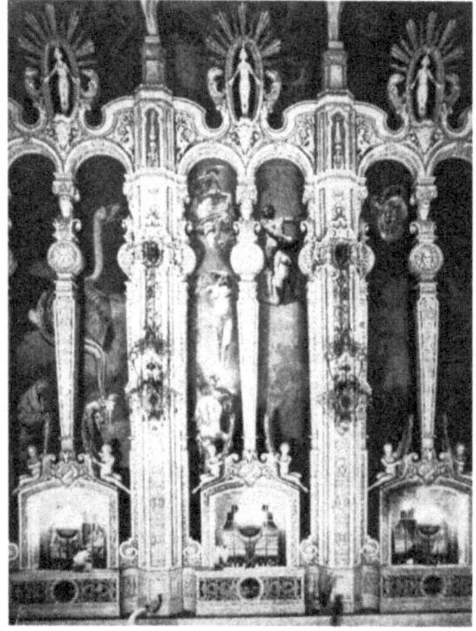
One thousand and one fantasies by Eberson in Chicago's Paradise Theatre.

MOVIE PALACES IN LOS ANGELES SET A NATIONAL TREND

Opening in 1911, and appearing much like an office building, except for the marquee and terracotta figures, the fourth and final palace in downtown Los Angeles for the Orpheum vaudeville circuit was its namesake, the Orpheum (today the Palace, at 630 South Broadway). The principal architect was G. Albert Lansburgh, who showed off his skill with Beaux Arts-inspired palazzo façades in a style created during the Italian Florentine Renaissance. The façade includes large polychromed terracotta standing figures by Domingo Mora, which depict the muse of music—a jester with a lute; of song—a female with a sheet of music; of dance—a ballerina; and of drama—a poet reading.

The architect of the Orpheum/Palace, G. Albert Lansburgh (1876–1969) was born in Panama, raised in San Francisco, and attended the

Eberson's atmospheric effect in Chicago's Paradise Theatre, 1928.

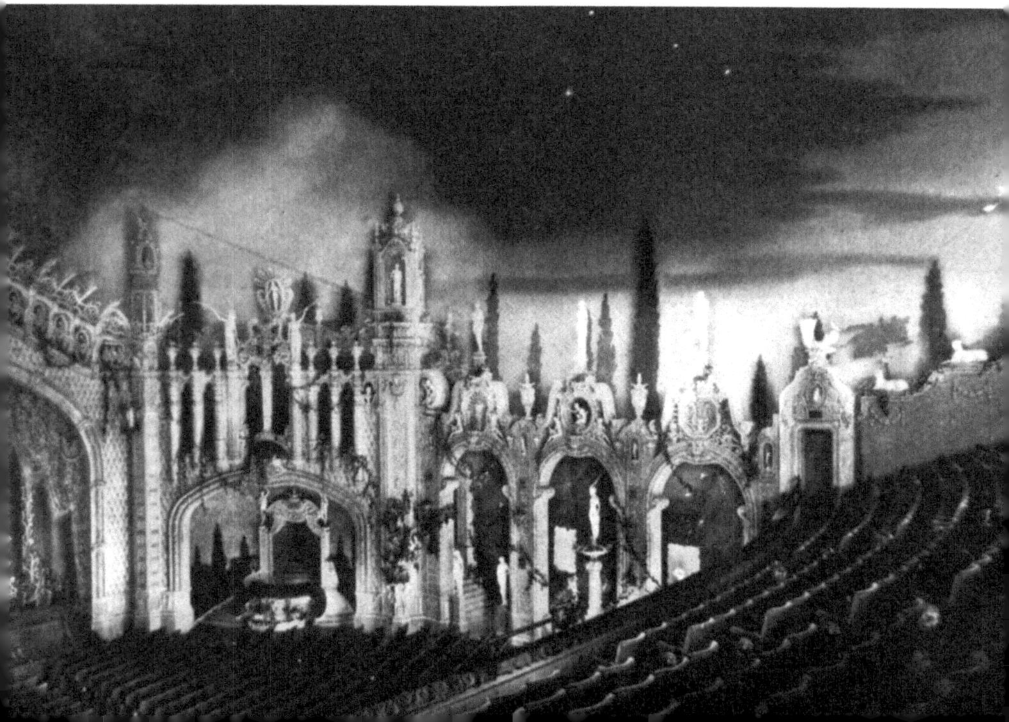

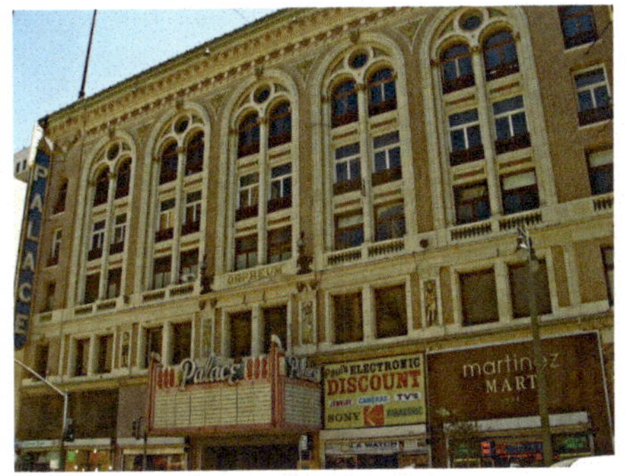

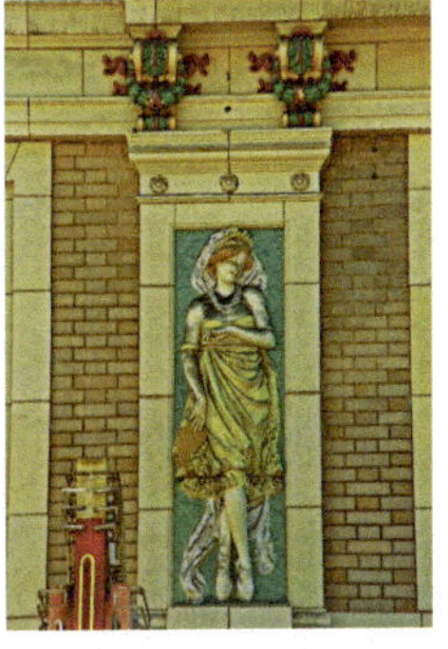

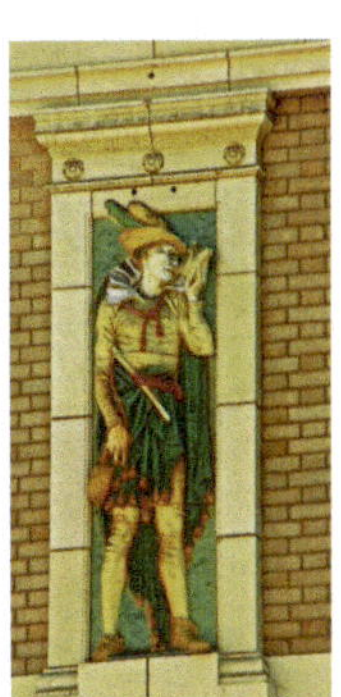

Above left: Lansburgh's Orpheum along Broadway in Los Angeles passes for an office building from the outside.

Above centre: Terracotta takes a colorful turn in Dance, one of four figures by Domingo Mora on the façade of the Orpheum in Los Angeles.

Above right: Drama, one of four exterior figures on the Orpheum by Domingo Mora.

University of California, Berkeley. He worked part-time in the offices of Bernard Maybeck before enrolling in the École des Beaux-Arts, Paris in 1901, earning a diploma five years later. He returned home to San Francisco a month after the great earthquake. Immediately he designed numerous buildings including a theatre for the San Francisco-based Orpheum Theatre circuit that eventually garnered him another fifty theatre commissions, then more for its successor, KAO (Keith-Albee-Orpheum) theatre chains, then their successor, RKO (Radio-Keith-Orpheum). RKO was formed when David Sarnoff of RCA engineered the merger of KAO and Joseph P. Kennedy's Film Booking Offices of America (FBO) under the control of Radio Corporation of American (RCA) in October 1928 to create a market for RCA's Photophone, sound-on-film technology. RKO's most famous titles are *King Kong* (1933) and *Citizen Kane* (1941).

Inside the Orpheum, Lansburgh used recessed lighting against reflectors in the three domes to glow across the ceiling. This glow became standard lighting procedure for later movie palaces. The theatre has gained new

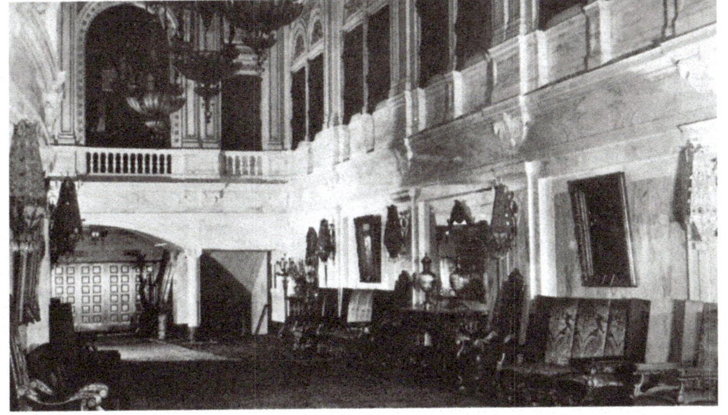

Unlike any office building, the Orpheum's foyer hints at what is to come.

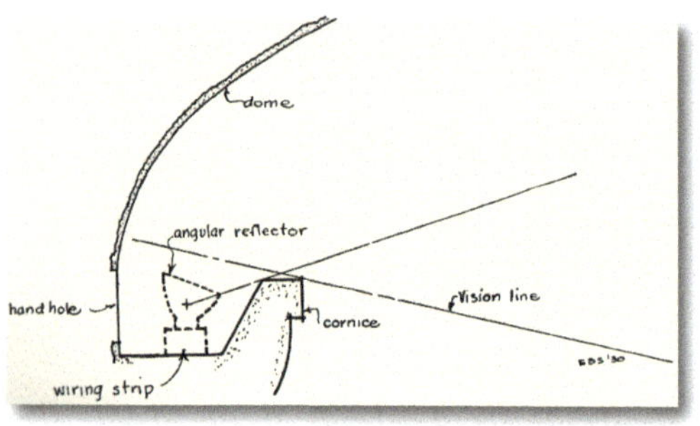

Recessed cove lighting designed by Lansburgh for the Orpheum in Los Angeles in 1926 became a standard.

importance with the discovery that Margaret Ianelli, along with her husband, Alphonso, designed posters for the Orpheum in 1914–15, before moving to Chicago.

The Orpheum became the Palace Theatre in 1926, shifting its primary entertainment to film, becoming the first, first-run movie palace to present sound films in southern California. At the time of the conversion to film, the box seats, a staple for live entertainment, were removed to give the screen clear sightlines. In 1926, large murals by Anthony Heinsbergen (1894–1981) took their place.

Born Antoon Heinsbergen in the Netherlands, young Anthony Heinsbergen settled, with his parents, in Los Angeles in 1906. After completing several mural commissions, he came to the attention of Alexander Pantages, who hired him to decorate one of his theatres. Soon Heinsbergen's company had grown to one hundred and eighty artists/painters who, paralleling the burst of theatre construction, completed over seven hundred and fifty murals across the United States. Today Anthony Heinsbergen is considered the dean of North American theatre mural painters.

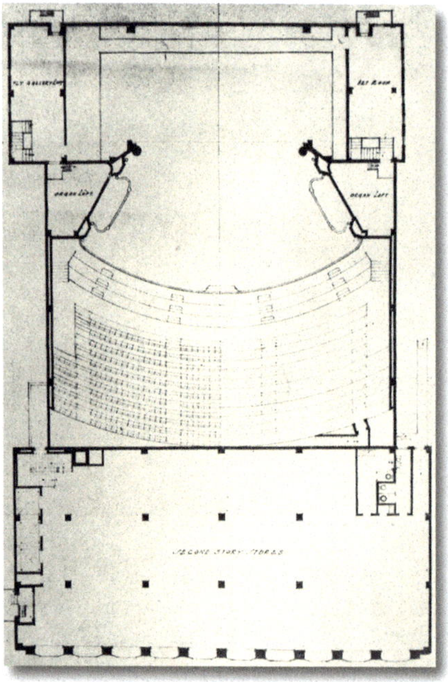

Box seats were a reminder of the Orpheum's live theatre days, before film.

PANTAGES GREEK

Starting in 1911, Alexander Pantages built his own theatres with his favorite architect, B. Marcus Priteca (1881–1971), who regularly worked with muralist Heinsbergen. Priteca's designs and Heinsbergen's murals created an exotic Neoclassical look that the industry named "Pantages Greek." Seating 2,703 and completed in 1930, The Pantages Theatre, formerly the RKO Pantages at the corner of Hollywood and Vine, in Hollywood, is the last theatre built by the Greek vaudeville and movie house impresario. Priteca designed it in an eclectic Classical style with a central staircase flanked by standing female figures, acting like muses to the young men kneeling before them, one with an airplane, another with a film camera. Large silver-leafed figures stand along the walls against undulating backdrops. Even for Hollywood this was high

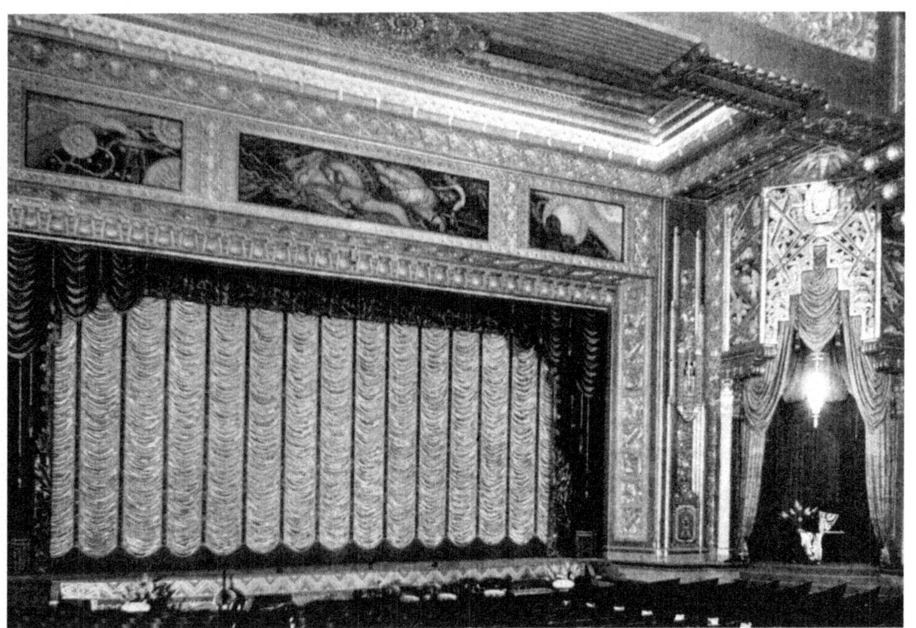

Classic Deco murals by Anthony Heinsbergen top the proscenium in the Pantages, Los Angeles.

theatrical style, which provided a striking counter to the Baroque Revival style championed by other moguls and adored by the public at the time.

Alexander Pantages (1867–1936) was born on the Greek island of Andros. He left home at the age of nine to spend two years at sea, then worked on the Panama Canal before moving to San Francisco, followed by several years in the Canadian mining-boom town of Dawson City. In 1902, Pantages had settled in Seattle, Washington and opened the Crystal Theatre, a vaudeville and motion-picture place. Two years later he opened a second theatre in Seattle, the Pantages, followed in 1906 by the Lois, named after his wife. By 1920, he owned more than thirty vaudeville theatres and controlled maybe sixty more. These formed the Pantages circuit.

Benjamin Marcus Priteca was born in Glasgow, Scotland in 1889. He graduated from the University of Edinburgh in 1907 and the Royal College of Fine Arts in 1909. Months later he arrived in Seattle. Along the way he became fascinated with the acoustical research of Wallace Sabine (1868–1919) of Harvard University. As a draftsman for E. W. Houghton (1856–1927) he met Alexander Pantages by chance in 1911. He would spend the next two decades as Pantages' personal architect. As Pantages expanded his theatre circuit, Priteca expanded his own practice as he drew inspiration from classical Greek, Roman and Renaissance architecture, as was his client's wont.

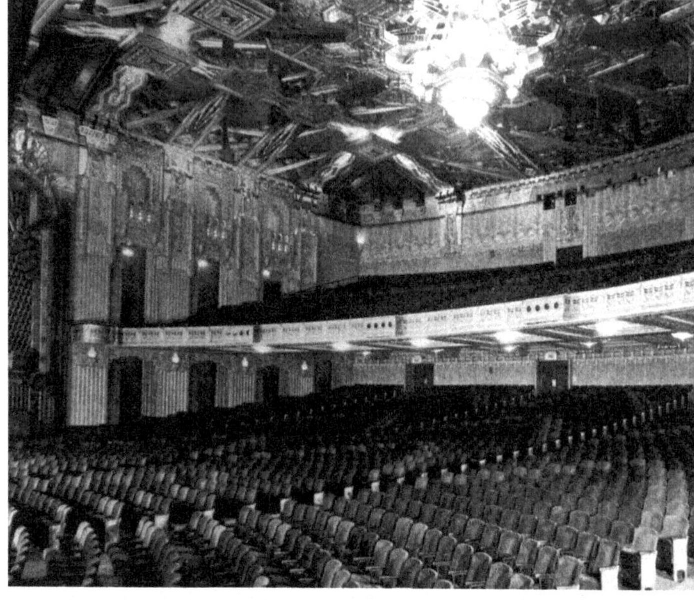

The auditorium ceiling in Hollywood's Pantages has complex patterns and one great chandelier.

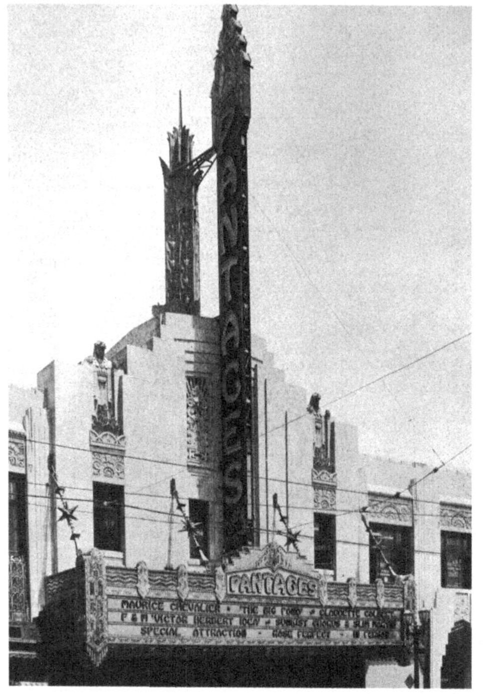

The marquee almost could not keep up with the interior decoration of the Hollywood Pantages Theatre.

The exterior of the buildings, often an office block or tower, was usually in brick and ornamental terracotta. Inside, the theatres were lavish. Pantages liked Roman columns left and right of the proscenium arch, heavy drapes and his favorite color scheme was ivory and gold. Priteca's most famous theatre was the Hollywood Pantages. At the opening, Priteca is quoted as saying that it would "best exemplify America of the moment. Effort centered upon motifs which were modern—never futuristic—yet based on time-tested classicism of enduring good taste and beauty." Holding the distinction of being the last movie palace of its kind to open in Hollywood, it was for years home of the Academy Award ceremonies.

By the late 1910s, Hollywood had surpassed Chicago as the nation's film production center, and to accommodate this new medium, Los Angeles converted

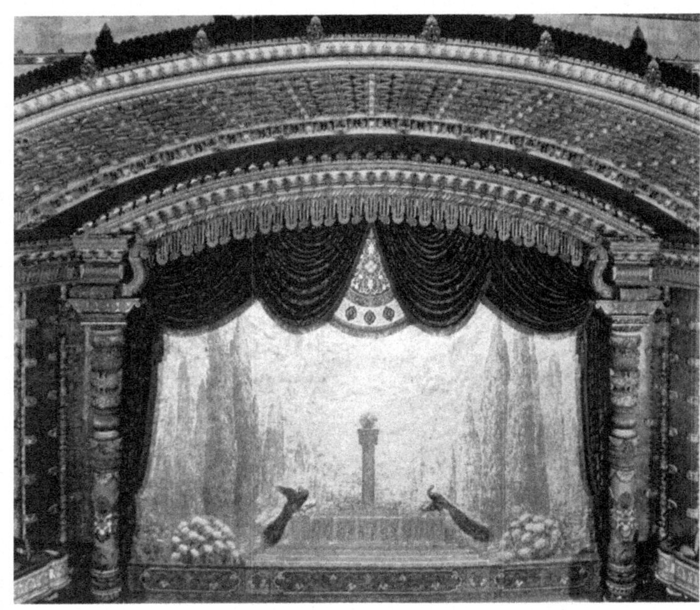

An almost modest stage in the El Capitan.

its great vaudeville houses into grand movie palaces and built new ones. Charles E. Toberman, the "Father of Hollywood," envisioned a downtown theatre district when he partnered with Sid Grauman to first open

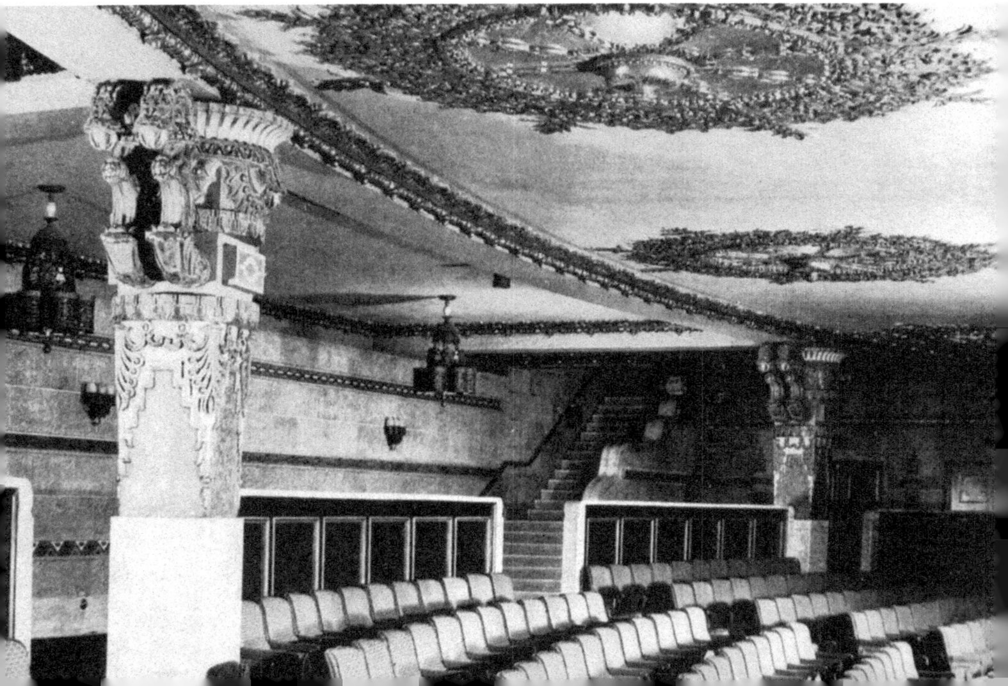

Column caps and lighting add exotica to the Los Angeles El Capitan.

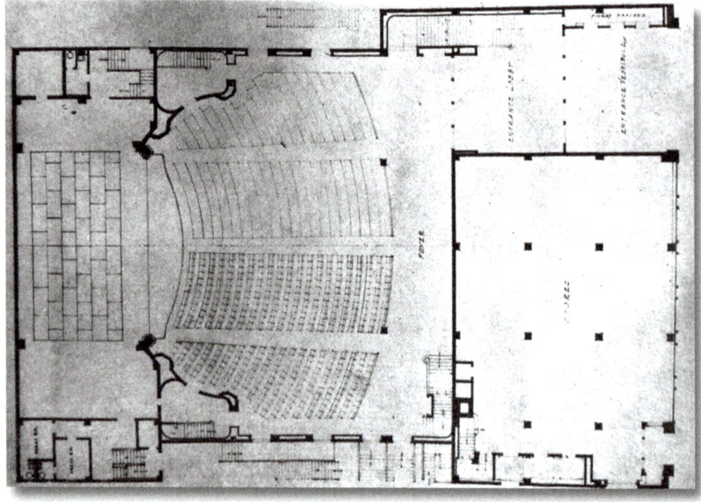

The main floor plan of the El Capitan in Los Angeles.

El Capitan, 6838 Hollywood Boulevard, in 1926 and then the Chinese Theatre the following year.

El Capitan's exterior façade is in a Spanish Colonial Revival-inspired style designed by Stiles O. Clements (1883–1966) of the architectural firm Morgan, Walls & Clements. Meanwhile E. Albert Lansburgh, who had become the go-to Los Angeles interior theatre architect, created the lavish East Indian-inspired interior.

After El Capitan presented the world premier of *Citizen Kane* in 1941, the theatre remained Paramount Pictures' primary west coast showcase until the US Supreme Court's anti-trust decision in "US vs. Paramount

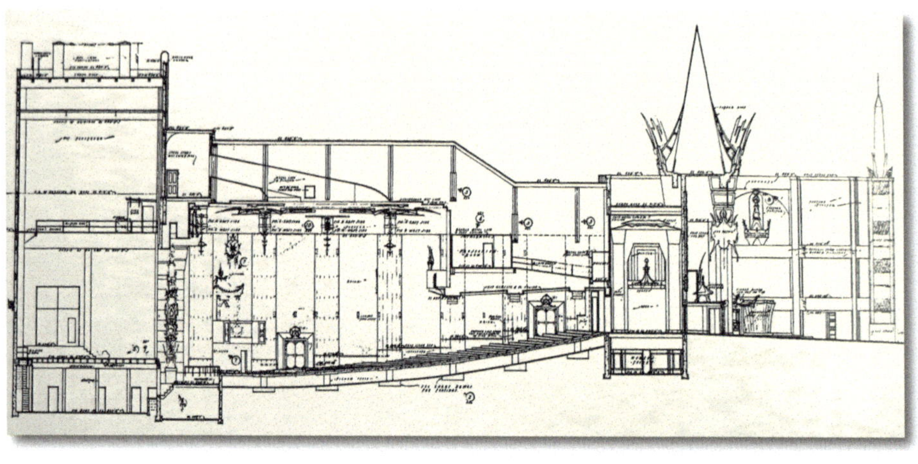

The architect's cross-section drawing of Grauman's Chinese shows how complicated movie theatre construction could be.

Pictures" forced Paramount to divest itself of its theatre holdings. Paramount survived, and is now the fifth oldest film studio in the world, behind Universal Studios, Nordisk Film, Pathé, and Gaumont Film Company. After a series of owners, El Capitan was acquired by the Walt Disney Company in 1989 and extensively remodeled back to its original look. The "new" theatre now features a 1929 Mighty Wurlitzer, originally from San Francisco's Fox Theatre.

Fulfilling the public's desire for the exotic, Grauman and Toberman—with shareholders Mary Pickford, Douglas Fairbanks and Howard Schenck—opened the 1,152-seat Chinese Theatre on May 18, 1927, at 6925 West Hollywood Boulevard with the premiere of Cecil B. DeMille's silent religious epic *The King of Kings*. Designed by Raymond M. Kennedy

At Grauman's Chinese, the audience sat inside a giant pagoda which wouldn't have looked out of place on a movie set.

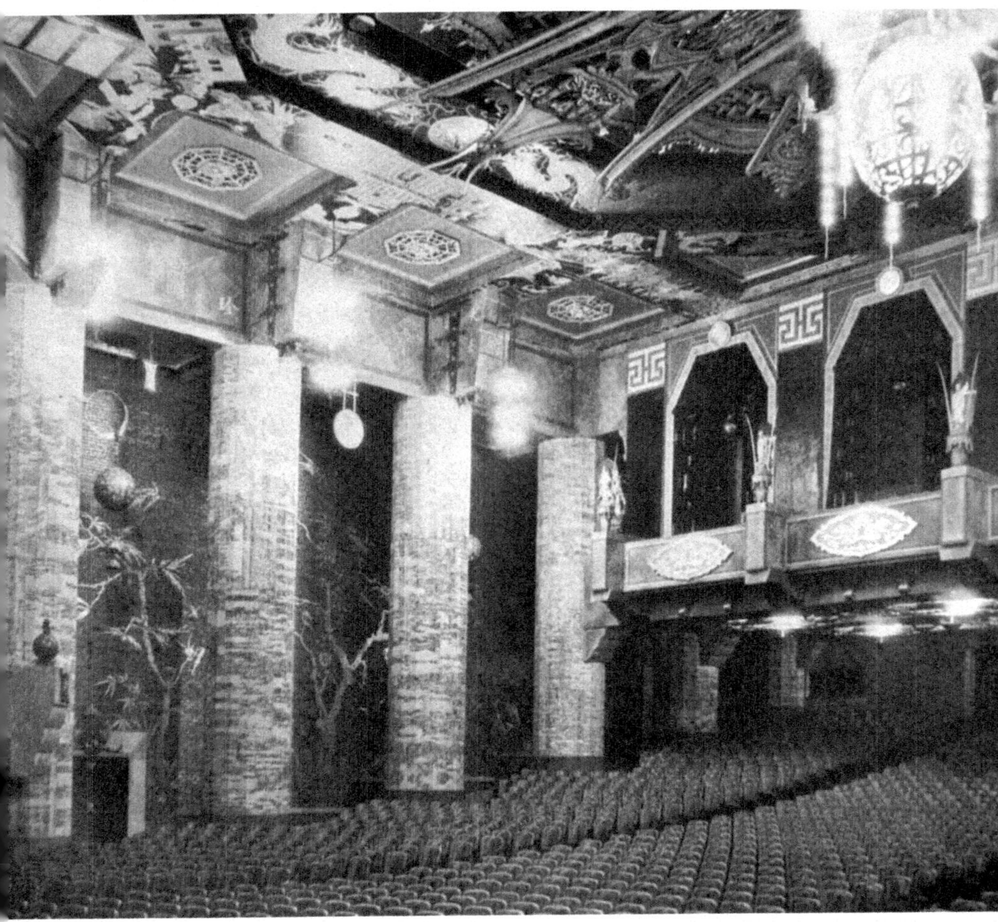

(1891–1976) of Meyer & Holler, it took some eighteen months to build this Chinese extravaganza. During construction, Grauman hired Jean Klossner to formulate extra-hard cement for the forecourt. It became the site of the footprint ceremony; first to make her mark was Norma Talmage, followed by Douglas Fairbanks and everyone else. This was a perfect marketing and branding ploy. The projection of larger than life images in exotic milieus led the public to accept that real people lived in this way too, and so movie stars were fantasized into existence. And what better way to realize a temporary screen image than with a permanent display of hands, feet and signatures in hard cement. In 1953,

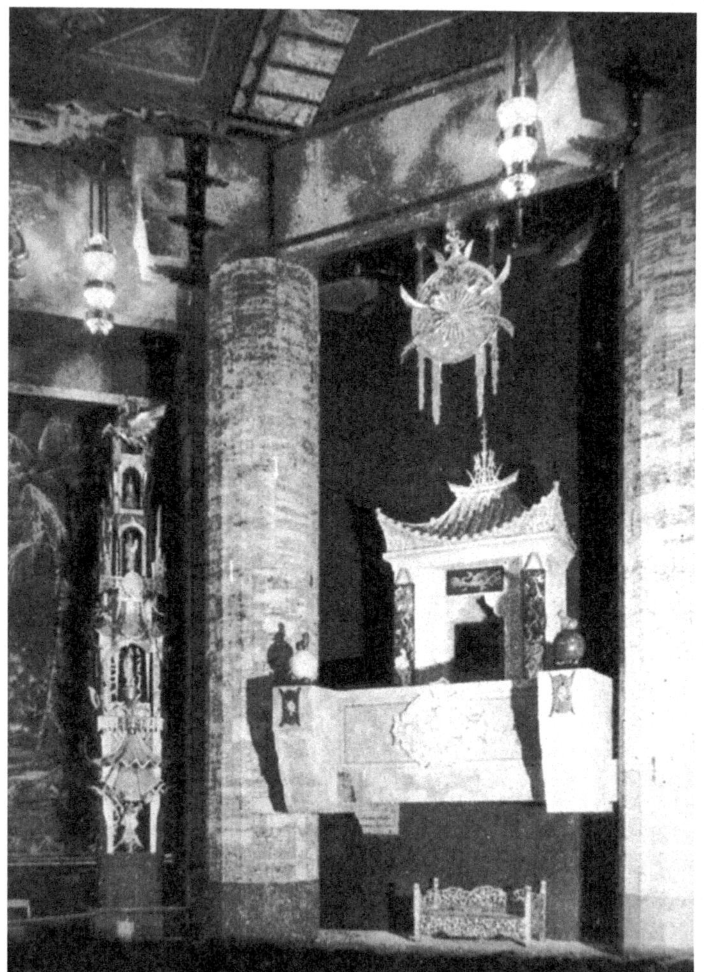

Even the box seats were enough for an emperor in Grauman's Chinese.

the walk of fame stars on the sidewalk of Hollywood Boulevard followed.

In 1926–27, H. L. Gumbiner (1879–1952), an independent film exhibitor from Chicago, commissioned the 900-seat Tower Theatre for a very narrow lot he owned at 802 S. Broadway in downtown Los Angeles from the architects S. Charles Lee (1899–1990) and Samuel Tilden Norton (1877–1959). It would be the first of several commissions by Gumbiner, and Lee's first independent commission.

Cover for sheet music from *King of Kings*.

S. Charles Lee was born Simon Charles Levi in Chicago in 1899, into a second generation of German-Jewish immigrants. In high school he built three automobiles, and then worked in the offices of Chicago theatre architect Henry Newhouse before attending Armour Institute of Technology to study the principles of the École des Beaux Arts, American style. After graduation he worked for Rapp & Rapp and witnessed the Tribune Tower competition before moving to Los Angeles.

To give the Tower Theatre more presence on its narrow corner, Lee chose the newly popular Baroque Revival style, which incorporated elements of ill-defined attribution—French, Spanish, Spanish-Moorish, and of course, Italian. Casting the cornucopia of styles in terracotta made them decidedly more affordable and suitable as popular decoration. When it opened, the Tower had murals by A. T. Heinsbergen, and was wired for talking pictures, but for most patrons it was the new air conditioning that was of unique importance, especially in Los Angeles summers. Both air conditioning and being wired for sound were firsts in Los Angeles, and the Tower benefitted from hosting a sneak preview and the Los Angeles premier of Warner Bros.' innovative part-talkie film *The Jazz Singer*, starring Al Jolson in October 1927.

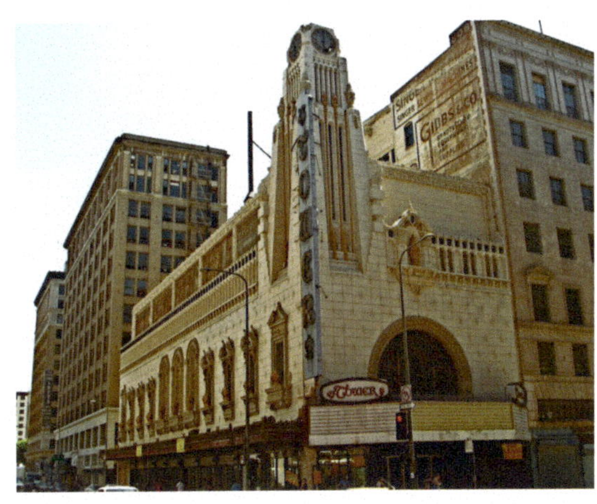

A sneak preview of *The Jazz Singer* at Tower Theatre made the public aware of this new theatre on Broadway in Los Angeles.

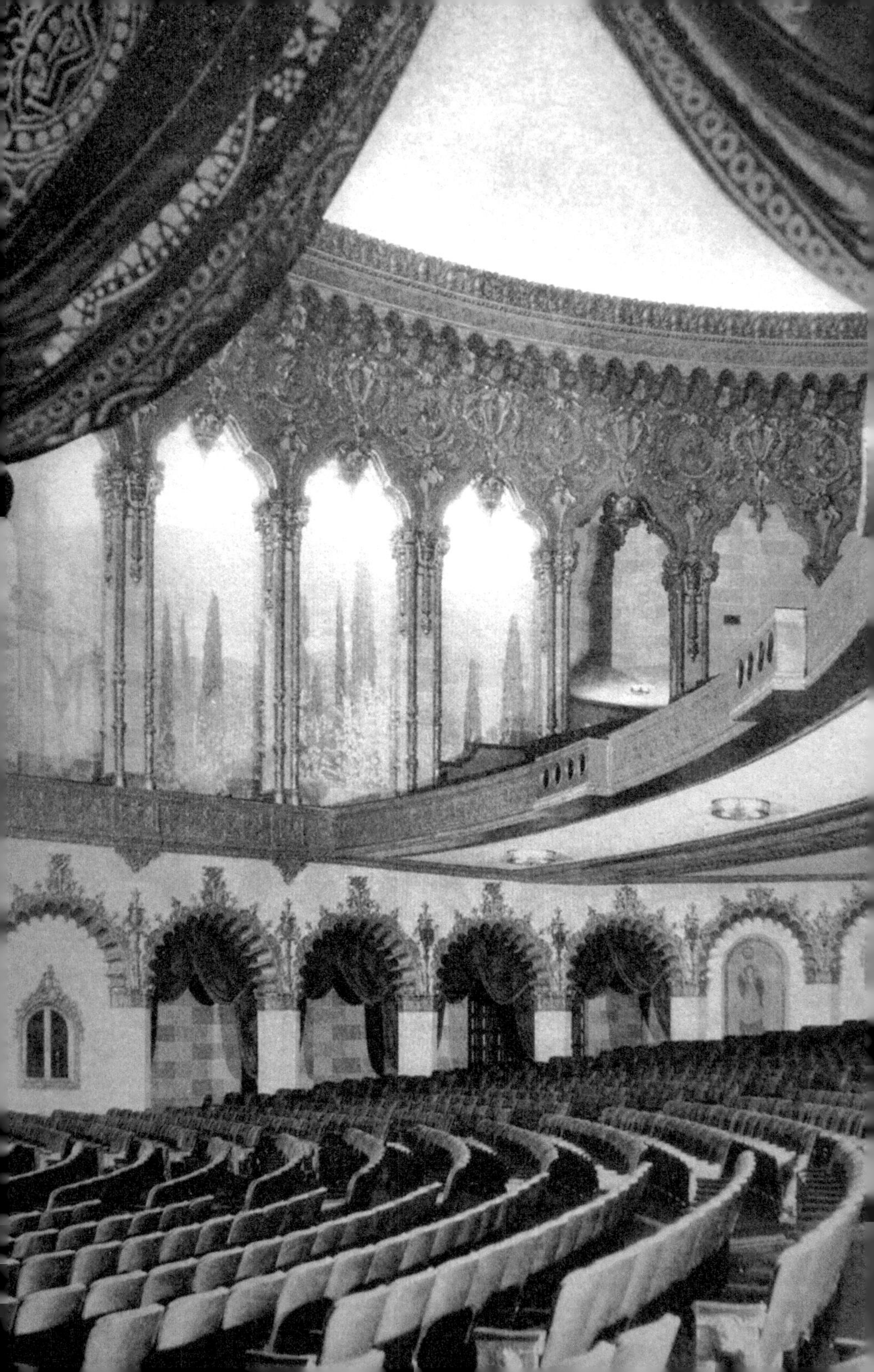

YOU AIN'T SEEN NOTHIN' YET

THE WONSKOLASER OR WONSAL BROTHERS—Harry (born Hirsz), Albert (born Aaron), Sam (born Szmul), and Jack (born Itzak or Jacob)—who emigrated with their parents from Russia (now Poland), started in the movie business in Pennsylvania with a film projector. By 1903 this had morphed into their first movie house, the Cascade, in New Castle, Pennsylvania. By 1916 they were known as the Warner Brothers and had made their first nationally syndicated film, *My Four Years in Germany*. In 1918, they opened Warner Brothers studio on Sunset Boulevard in Hollywood and finally formally incorporated on April 4, 1923. While other studios had female and male stars, it was a French male German Shepherd, Rin Tin Tin (1918–32), who brought the studio its first star and immediate success. Rinty (his nickname) also brought success to Darryl F. Zanuck (1902–79) from Wahoo, Nebraska, who played a major role in the Hollywood studio system that made stars glamorous and movie palaces a necessity. In 1927, Warner Bros. released *The Jazz Singer*, a "talkie" in which Al Joson said, "You ain't seen nothin' yet."

In 1933 Zanuck left Warner Bros. to found 20th Century Films with Joseph Schenck and William Goetz. They released their films through United Artists. In 1935 Zanuck bought out Fox to became 20th Century Fox. The big five studios were now all interrelated.

In the 1920s, the building codes for the city of Los Angeles allowed for two types of theatre construction, based on the distinction between live drama and motion-picture presentations in the nickelodeon style. The motion picture ordinance was written for theatres of up to nine hundred seats, prescribed as one-story wood or masonry structure with a wooden roof, allowing for neither stage nor balcony. The legitimate theatre ordinance, on the other hand, allowed for a full stage and balcony, requiring Class A steel-reinforced construction. The solution for the theatre Charles Lee was commissioned to build was a conflation of the two. Lee submitted his plans for a narrow nine-hundred seat Class A steel-reinforced motion-picture theatre with balcony, narrow 7-foot stage and no fly loft. The city's Building and Safety Commission, not understanding his hybrid, rejected it. An appeal

Opposite: A circular auditorium by G. Albert Lansburgh gave the Warner in Los Angeles distinction.

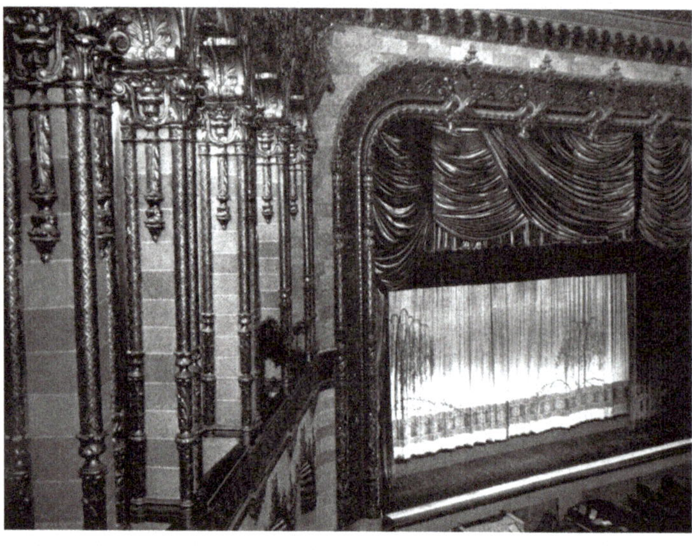

The Warner Bros.'s Warner Theatre stage in Los Angeles was traditional—their films were not.

to the city attorney, who said it was legal if unorthodox, convinced the Building and Safety Commission to approve it. On the inside, the Tower was a miniature Paris Opera, a style everyone could relate to, and feel suitably Parisian and decadent in.

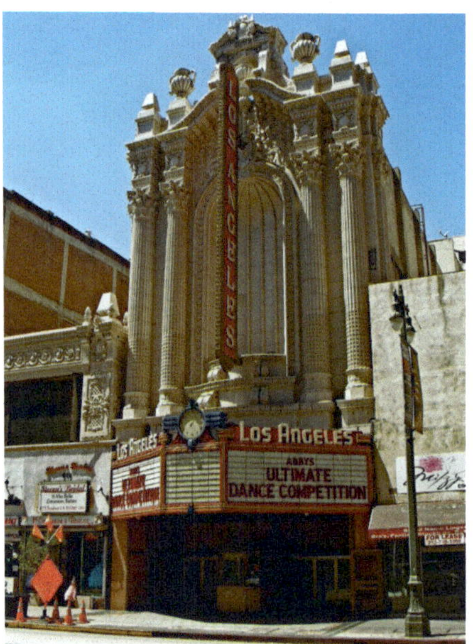

The Los Angeles is a Spanish Baroque inspiration in terracotta. The marquee looks to be an afterthought.

H. L. Gumbiner commissioned a second theatre from Lee, the 2,000-seat Los Angeles (1930–31) at 615 S. Broadway, but before he started on it Gumbiner and Lee toured the major motion-picture theatres of the United States to see what others were doing and noticed a general popularity of French Renaissance and Baroque styles. Not confronting what they saw as a national trend, the Los Angeles filtered visions gleaned from Versailles.

BRAVURA LEADS THE WAY TO PROFITS

When Los Angeles movie-going crowds revelled in Grauman's hyperbole and inspired views of history's exotic sides of architecture, they were following along a trail blazed by Chicagoans Balaban and Katz, who in turn seem to have been inspired by Gründerzeit architecture found in German-speaking urban

Europe between the 1880s and the first decade of the twentieth century. This architecture was not itself a revival of a specific past style such as Classical, Gothic, Italian, Northern or French Renaissance, or Baroque and Rococo from anywhere, but a permanent compressing of them with a spicy measure of Chinese, Persian and Mughal Indian forms to create an otherworldly visual mix. Versions of this mélange were revived by Balaban and Katz in their terracotta Spanish Baroque-inspired or lush Louis XIV/XV/XVI-inspired, or quaint Mediterranean piazza or Persian courtyard-lined auditoria, all providing visceral pleasure for the senses, not the intellect.

Bravura defined Abraham Joseph Balaban (1889–1962), the showman, his brother Barney (1887–1971), the financial wizard, and Morris Katz (1869–?) and his son Sam (1893–?), who founded Balaban & Katz (B&K) in 1916 in Chicago. Within a decade Balaban & Katz had become a national motion-picture chain, renowned for the basics that today define the great age of movie palaces—singularly large terracotta façades with large encrusted windows serving as altar-portals into interiors of regal splendors; theatres of unprecedented size in congested urban locations; and, most important, profitable theatres.

The Balabans were born on the west side of Chicago. They quickly developed into showmen when they acquired a nickelodeon, and in 1913 they opened the city's first movie theatre with a balcony, the Circle Theatre at Kedzie and Roosevelt.

Balaban & Katz served only movies. Their audience was enveloped in film, plaster, draperies, murals and light, becoming living actors to the celluloid ones on the screen. Each paying customer became a character, an actor with her own stage every time she entered the theatre. The crowd's presence confirmed that the theatre and the film were real. Balaban & Katz theatres were enormous, large enough for a whole town to see a film together and have the necessary amenities before, during and after a performance. While Lamb had made his theatres stand out visually in the New York crowd, Balaban & Katz had succeeded by making theirs trusted destinations.

By the early 1920s Chicago's Loop was very congested. Balaban & Katz's solution was to build where people had recently moved to, where the expanded elevated transportation system ended. B&K proved that there was life for the movies out of the Loop. In keeping with their marketing strategy, only their Chicago Theatre stood in the Loop. Balaban and Katz gave their ticket buyers extravagant service, live musical productions before, between and after the film, and probably the most popular luxury: air conditioning throughout. Balaban and Katz's marketing strategy changed the way cinemas were built and operated nationwide, then around the world.

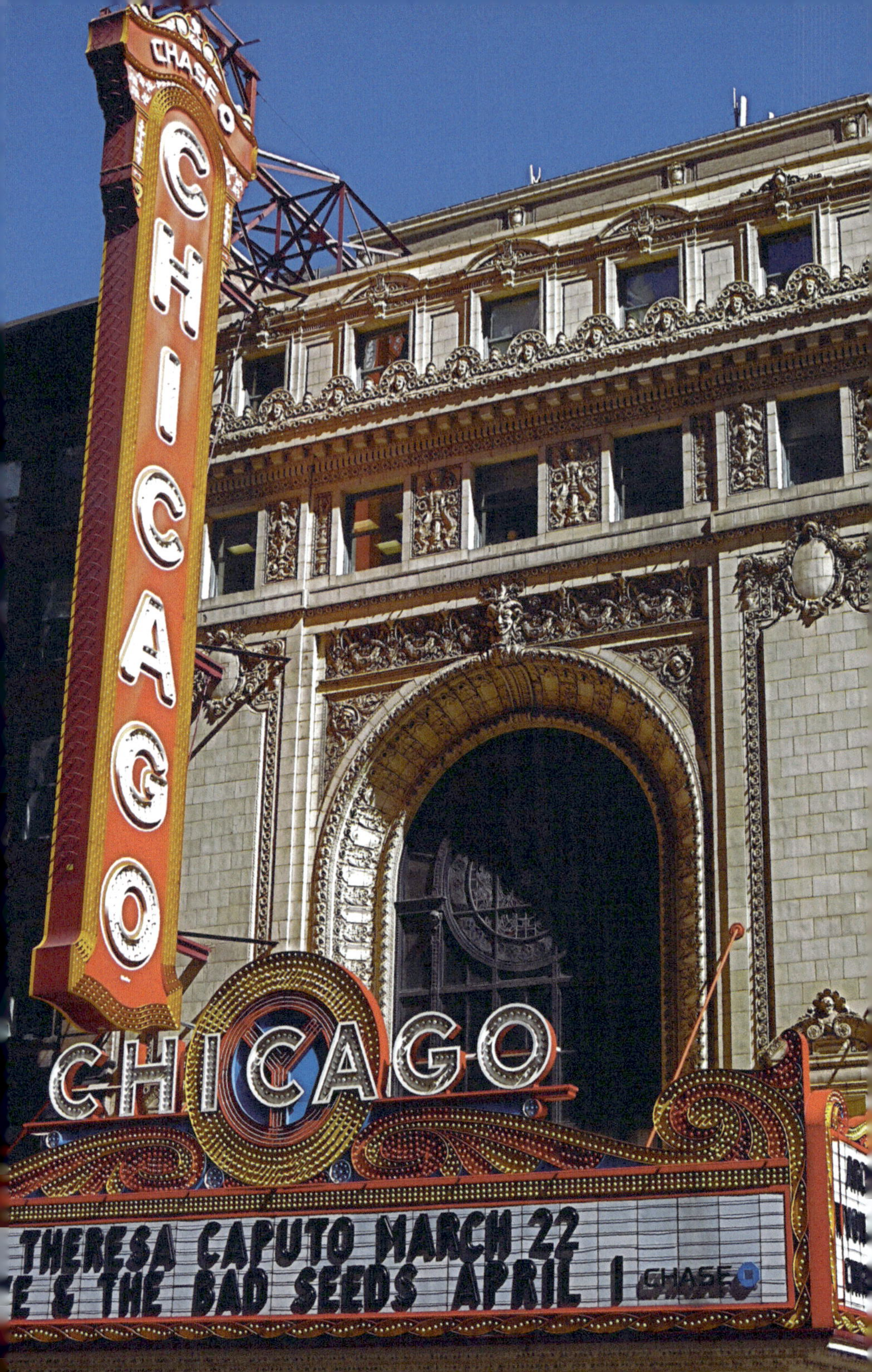
CHASE
CHICAGO
CHICAGO
THERESA CAPUTO MARCH 22
E & THE BAD SEEDS APRIL 1
CHASE

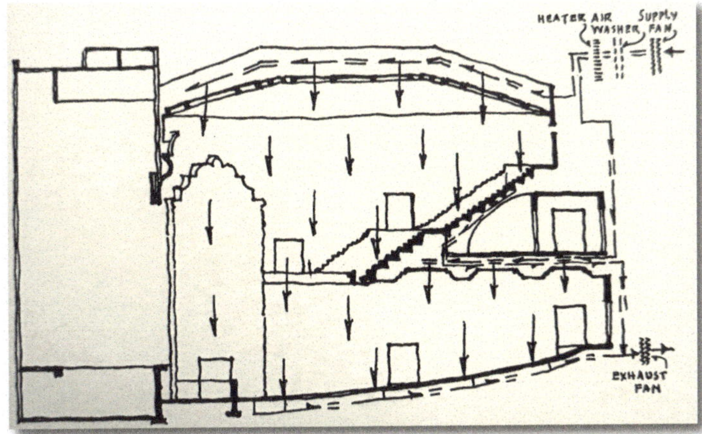

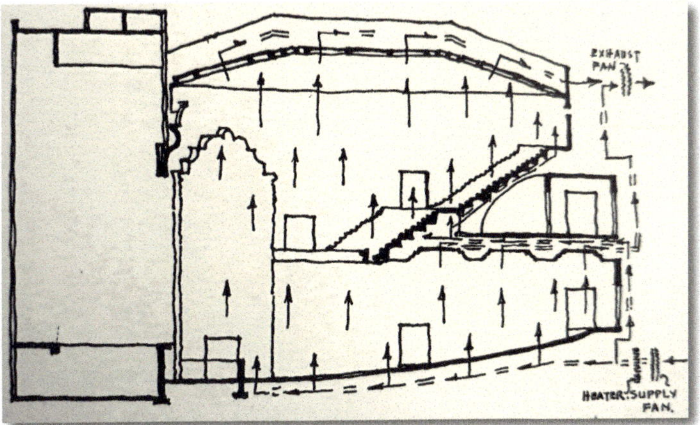

Balaban & Katz and other movie palaces featured clean air circulation. These illustrations show the air circulation, part of the early air conditioning system.

In 1925, Famous Players-Lasky Corporation bought a controlling interest in the corporation and Sam Katz became president of its Publix theaters. In 1946 federal action took apart the vertical integration of the film industry and in 1948 Famous Players-Lasky was folded into United Paramount Theatres with Barney Balaban eventually becoming its president.

Designed as the "Balaban and Katz Theatre," the Chicago opened in 1921 at 175 North State Street, the first movie palace built in the Loop and flagship of the B&K chain of theatres. It was designed by Cornelius W. Rapp and George L. Rapp, also known as Rapp & Rapp, in an extravagant faux French Baroque-inspired miscellany of the styles of Louis XIV/XV/XVI, at a reported cost of some four million dollars. Riffing on Louis became Rapp & Rapp's signature and provided easy steps for every man to historic erudition, especially where an authentic structure did not block the way. The public

Opposite: The Chicago Theatre was the only Balaban & Katz movie palace in the Loop. The marquee is new.

loved the Chicago and claimed it as the city's go-to film theatre. For years it was the leader among B&K's theatres.

The exterior of the Chicago features a 60-foot-wide, six-story-tall creamy terracotta façade around a great central window, which could have been snitched from the top row of Borromini's Palazzo Barberini in Rome. Balaban and Katz claimed the keystone with their own coat of arms—two horses holding ribbons of 35mm film in their jaws, outlined by film reels. Northwest Terra Cotta Company of Chicago provided the façade. The marquee was rebuilt in 1994 to look like its immediate predecessor, which did not look like the original.

Inside, the mélange of faux French Renaissance and Baroque thickened. Rapp & Rapp had visions of the royal chapel at Versailles when they designed the mezzanine and balcony of the grand lobby, and seem to have thought

The McNaulty Brothers, who designed the foyer of the Chicago Theatre, were masters of illusion. The plaster and Bohemian crystal looks French, but was made in Chicago.

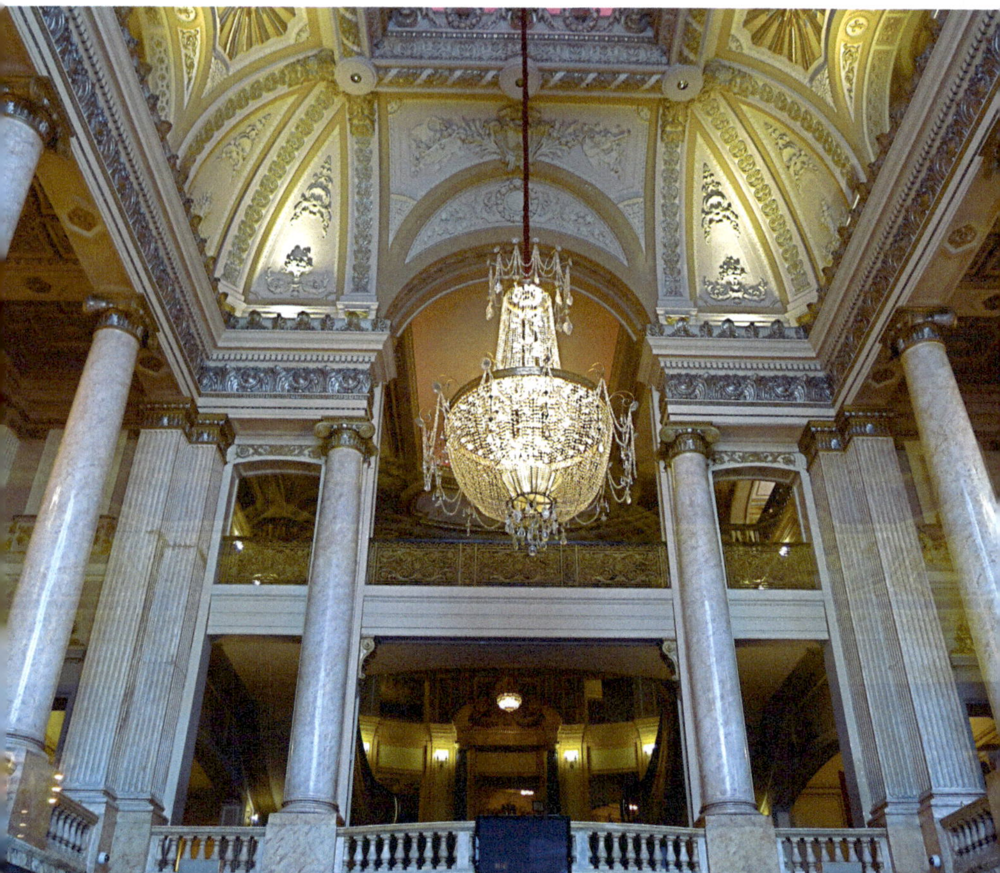

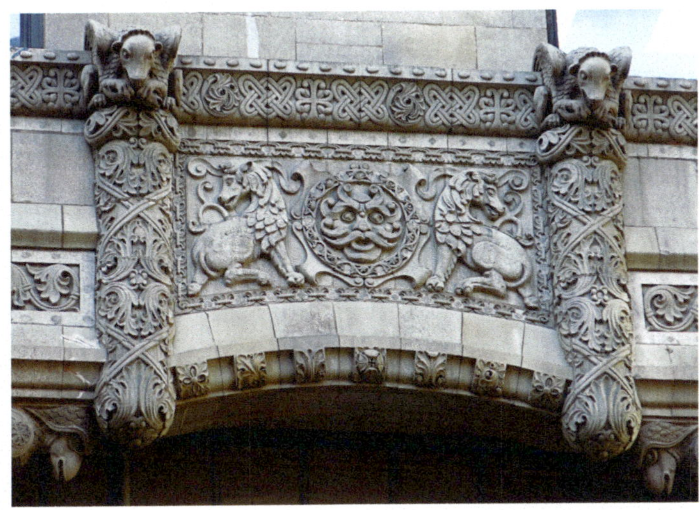

Terracotta medieval European demons and lions protect the oriental exotica inside the Oriental Theatre, Chicago.

of Garnier's Paris Opera, opened in 1875, for their grand staircase. Of course it helped if you had never been to either. Marshall Fields supplied much of the interior decoration, including the drapes and furniture as well as paintings on the walls. McNaulty Bros. provided faux Baroque plasterwork throughout. Crystal chandeliers and bronze fixtures are fitted with Steuben glass shades built by Victor Pearlman and Co., Chicago. Louis Grell, born Ludwig Heinrich Grell, III, to a German immigrant family in Council Bluffs, Iowa (1887–1960), painted fourteen large French fairytale murals on the proscenium arch in 1920, and then in 1932, fourteen Greek- and Roman-themed murals celebrating the Chicago World's Fair. At the time, the theatre's publicists called it "The Wonder Theatre of the World." Today, it is the oldest example of this style of theatre, as conceived by Rapp & Rapp.

When the Chicago opened on October 26, 1921, 3,861 seats were filled to see Norma Talmadge in First National Pictures' *The Sign on the Door*, a fifty-piece orchestra, a live stage show, and to hear famed organist

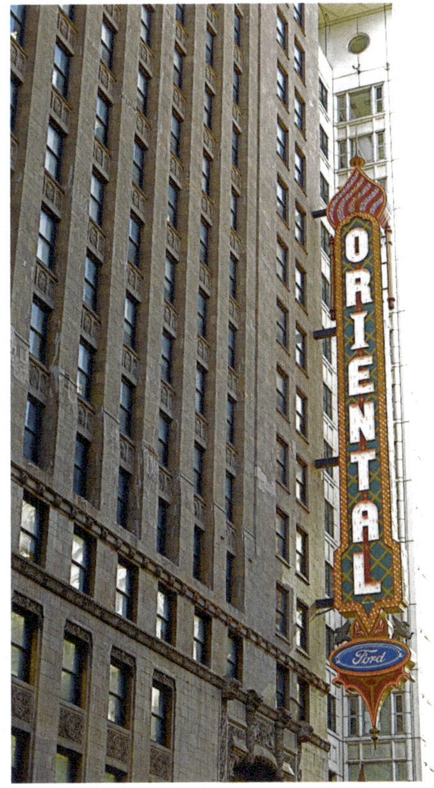

The marquee announces the Oriental to be in a skyscraper.

Jesse Crawford (1895–1962) at the 29-rank Wurlitzer organ. Usually a Mighty Wurlitzer took the place of an orchestra, but in the Chicago it augmented it. Between 1915 and 1933, over 7,000 Mighty Wurlitzers were installed in American movie theatres. Fewer than forty originals remain in operation.

BALABAN AND KATZ SERVED EXOTICA TO A WILLING PUBLIC

Just around the corner from the Chicago, the Oriental Theatre is "tucked" inside and behind the ground floor of a skyscraper at 24–28 West Randolph Street, on the site of the former Iroquois Theatre, where a disastrous fire in

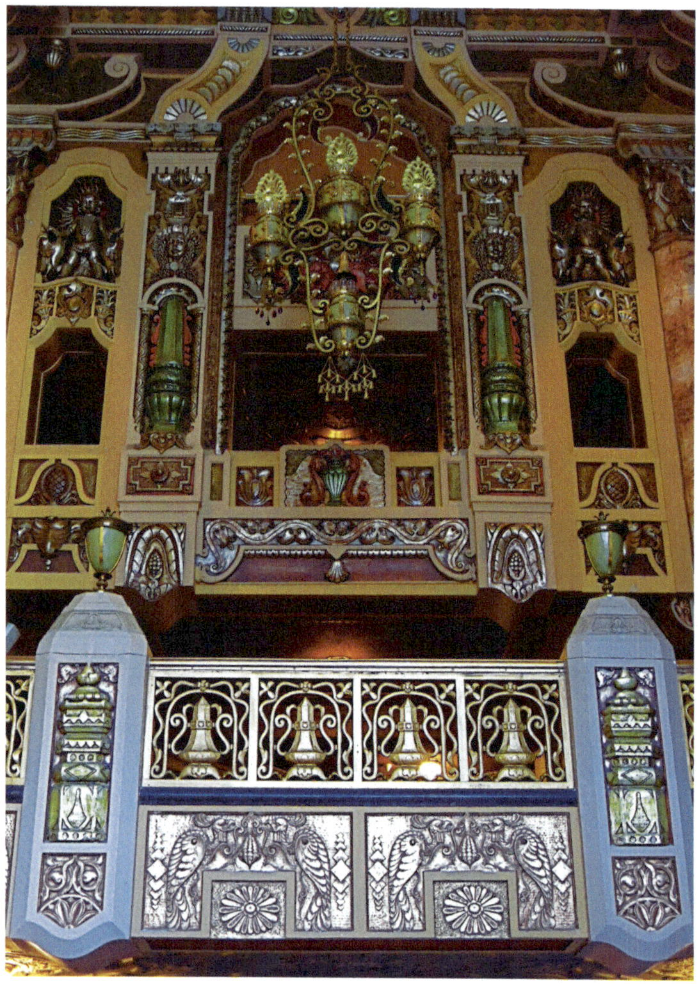

Welcome to a foyer of faux at the Oriental in Chicago. The elaborate orientalia gives definition to the theatre's name.

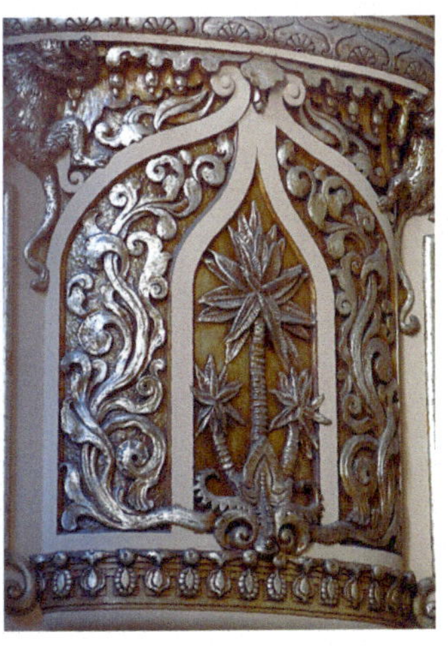

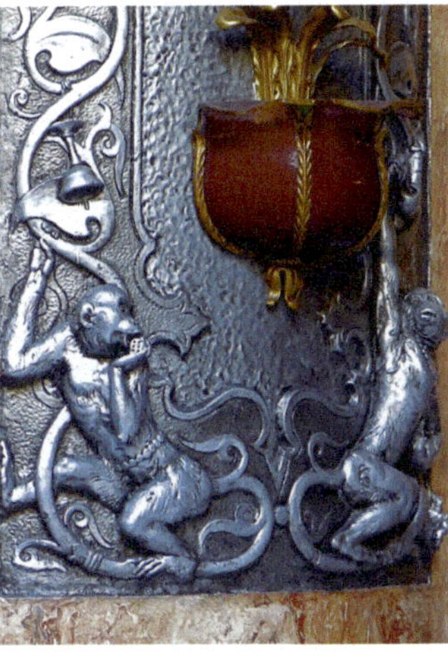

Far left: A faux balcony from nowhere.

Left: Aluminum-leafed monkeys at serious play.

1903 claimed 602 lives and changed the way theatres were designed. Designed by Rapp & Rapp and seating 3,217, the Oriental opened on May 9, 1926, and the interior is truly appropriate—oriental, as in far away India. Operated by B&K, the Oriental was both a movie and vaudeville house until the early 1930s, with performances of Duke Ellington and his orchestra a main attraction. In 1930, the film *Flight Commander* (aka *The Dawn Patrol*) attracted a record 124,985 paying customers in one week.

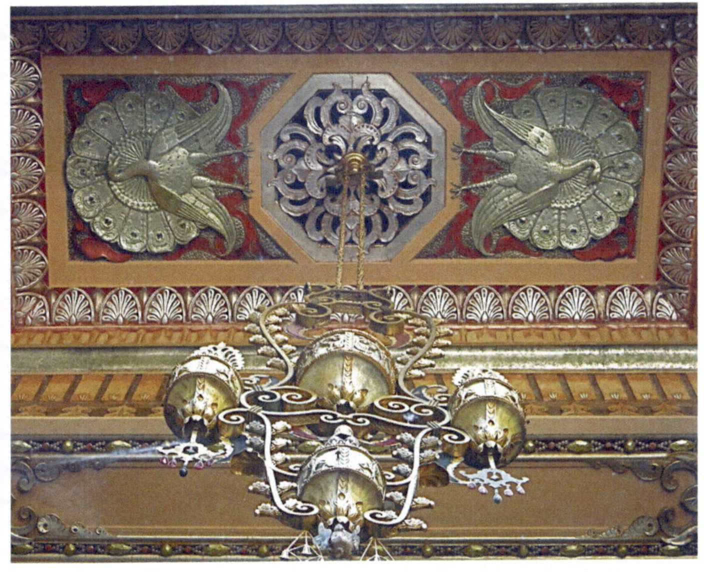

Even a pair of Persian peacocks standing on an air vent are found in faux in the Oriental.

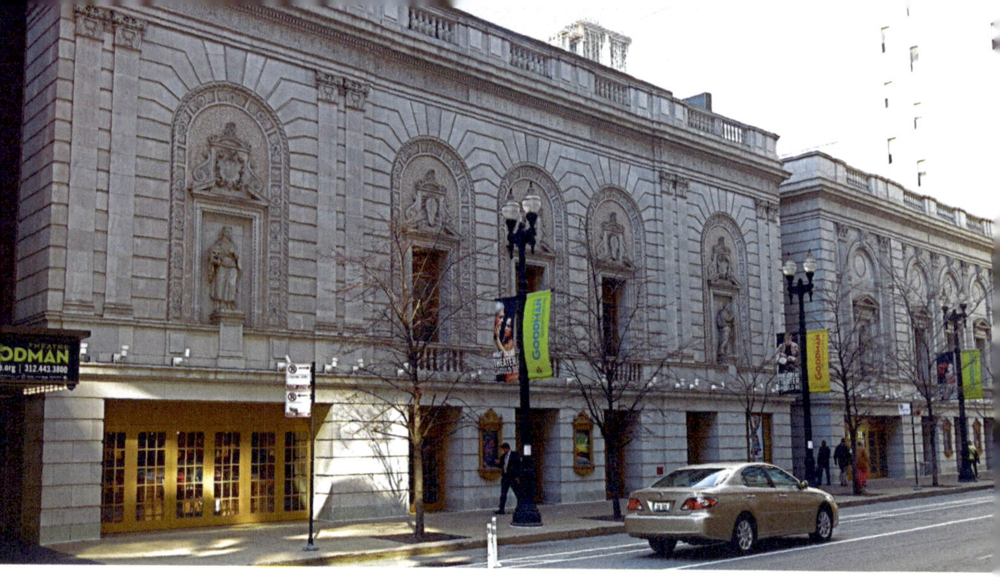

Chicago's Harris & Selwyn Twin Theatres, 1922, by C. Howard Crane for Sam H. Harris and Edgar Selwyn, are part of the Goodman Theatre today.

While the Oriental was a hot spot for movie goers, there were five or six other movie palaces in the immediate neighborhood. Almost next door along Randolph Street was the Woods; across the street the United Artists; around another corner the Michael Todd (originally the Selwyn & Harris double theatre); and two blocks west, the Bismark. The Loop was for movies and each of the big five studios had its own theatre there.

The last films were shown in the Oriental in the early 1970s and the venue was closed to the public in 1981. For some time its prime location was seriously considered for a two-story 50,000-square-foot shopping mall with a 1,600-seat cinema. Luckily less mercenary minds prevailed over the next fifteen years. In 1996, Chicago mayor Richard M. Daley announced that the Oriental would be restored to its original grandeur for the presentation of live stage musicals. Renamed the Ford Center for the Performing Arts in 1997, interior restoration was completed in October 1998, and it reopened with the Chicago premier of *Ragtime*.

A couple years after the Chicago Oriental opened, Maury I. Diggs, who also designed San Quentin Prison, shared credit with San Francisco architects Weeks and Day for the 2,800-seat Fox Oakland Theatre, at 1819 Telegraph Avenue, Oakland. On October 27, 1928, a staff of 150 welcomed its opening night patrons. To bring the curious public to its newest showplace, the operator paid fares for one hour preceding the opening of the Fox Oakland for all passengers on any of the 200 inbound cars and forty-three buses within the system's 7-cent fare zone. Described by the *San Francisco Chronicle* as "typical of the Brahamanicao temple of Northern India," the Fox Oakland's four-story stylized Hindu tower or *sikhara* may have helped some visualize that "San Francisco is the gateway to the Orient and the wonderful country of India," but the tower and façade were confusing enough that others wanted to name it "the Baghdad" because of what they saw as Middle Eastern influenced architecture. Then, in a reality check, instead of looking east for its name, it looked to the president of the West Coast Theatre chain who named it "West Coast Oakland." The Oakland became the 251st theatre to open in the West Coast Theatre chain.

To make the new West Coast Oakland even more visible, a special bevelled-glass ball containing 125 feet of orange-red tubing producing the equivalent of 20,000 watts of incandescent lighting marked the building for passing airplanes. Inside, *Goddess of Fire*, a mural by famed American western painter Maynard Dixon (1875–1946), greeted patrons from the upper wall opposite the entrance.

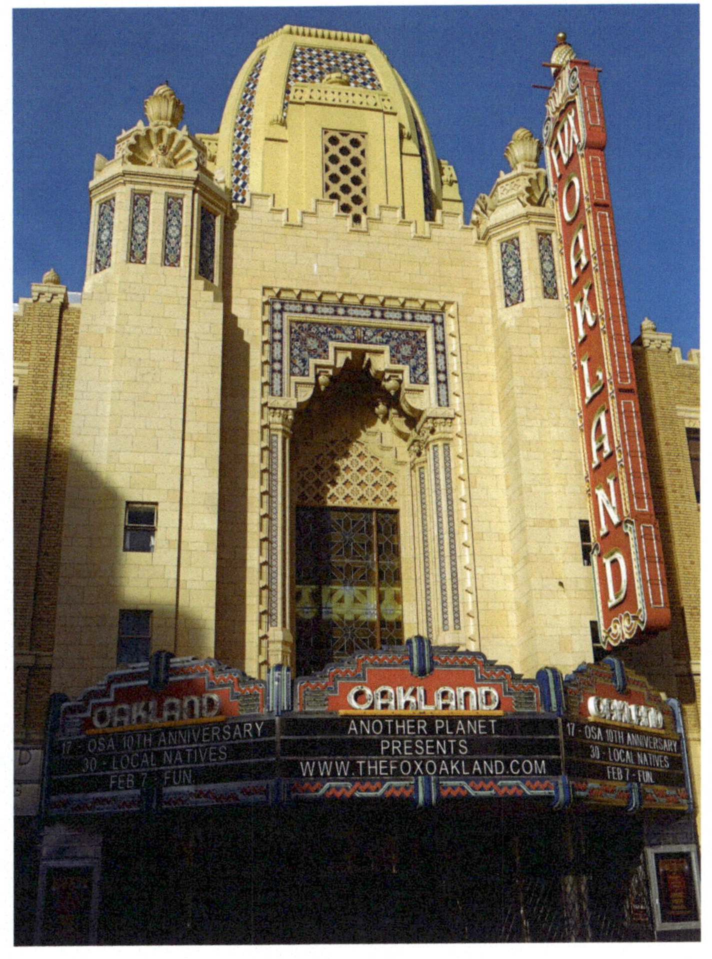

In the Fox Oakland Muslim India meets the Orient facing west of Oakland.

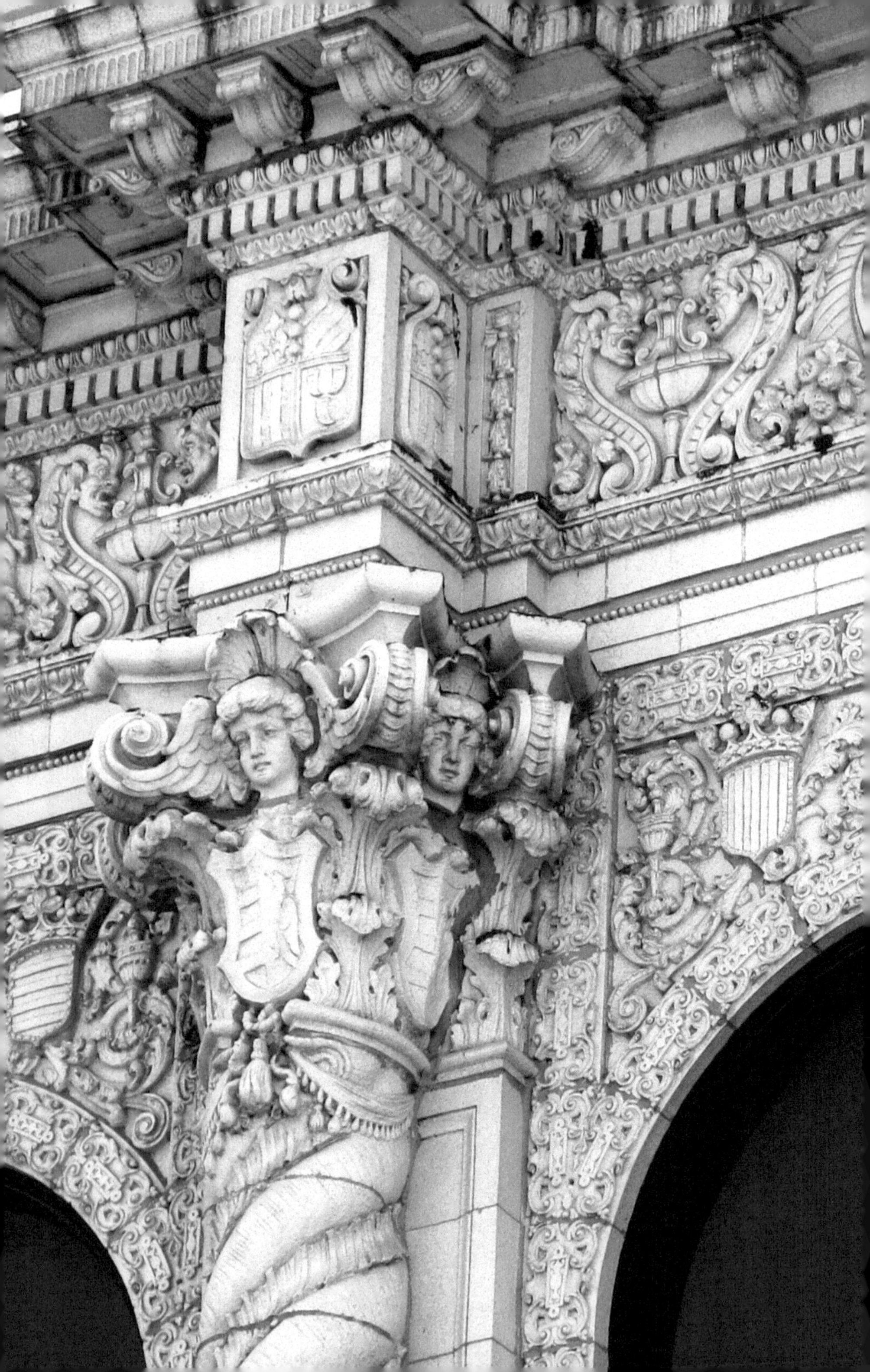

MOVIES BECOME TALKIES

WILLIAM FOX (1879–1952) was born in Tulchva (Tolcsva), Austria-Hungary, as Wilhelm Fried. By 1904 he had purchased his first nickelodeon. Within a decade he had become an independent exhibitor and distributor who led the successful fight against the Motion Picture Patents Company which at the time was monopolizing the industry. In 1915, he founded Fox Film Corporation, which in 1935 merged with 20th Century to become 20th Century Fox studios. At the time, each studio had a film star; some had two or three. Fox had Theda Bara, a very popular American silent film and stage actress whose *femme fatale* roles helped make her one of film's earliest sex symbols.

In one of the biggest deals ever transacted in show business, in 1929 William Fox acquired all 255 theatres of the West Coast Theatre circuit, appraised at $100 million. He later added to his string the famous Roxy Theatre in New York. Eventually, Fox controlled an estimated $165 million worth of entertainment.

In 1925, Fox purchased the American rights to the Tri-Ergon system—invented by three Germans, Josef Engl (1893–1942), Hans Vogt (1890–1979) and Joseph Massolle (1889–1957) and patented in 1919—and the Movietone sound-on-film inventions of Theodore Case (1888–1944) which debuted in 1927 with F. W. Murnau's film, *Sunrise (A Song of Two Humans)*. *Sunrise* was one of the first films with a soundtrack of music and sound effects. At the same time Fox introduced Movietone News, the first commercially successful sound film. At the time Fox proclaimed: "no second of every 24 hours passes but that the name of William Fox is on the screen in some part of the world." Converting theatres to sound was expensive, and Fox tried to convert his theatres—over 1,000 of them—all at once, then had an automobile accident, tried to buy out Marcus Loew, met the Great Depression, lost control of Fox Film Corporation, and lost a government anti-trust suit all in a short period of time. In a word, he was overwhelmed. His empire crumbled. Fox went bankrupt in 1936 and served six months in prison. He never recovered, but his five great Fox theatres remain glorious symbols of the great age of movie palaces.

Opposite: Hand-carved Mexican Spanish Baroque comes no finer than this terracotta façade on the former Diversey Theatre.

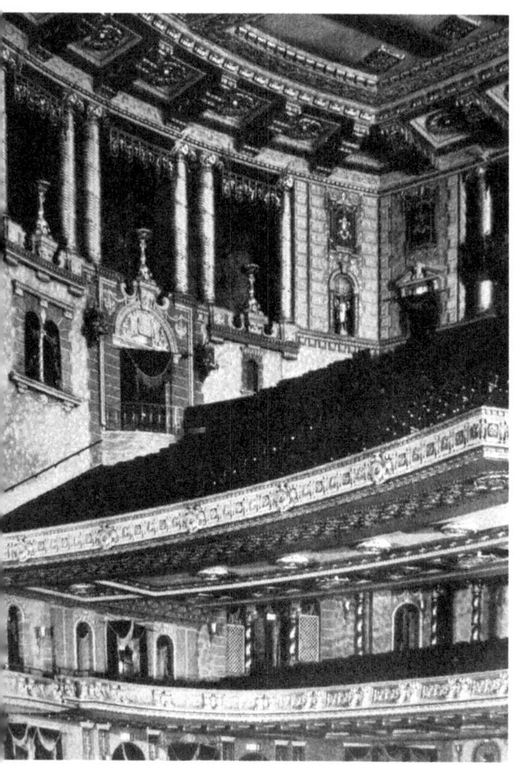

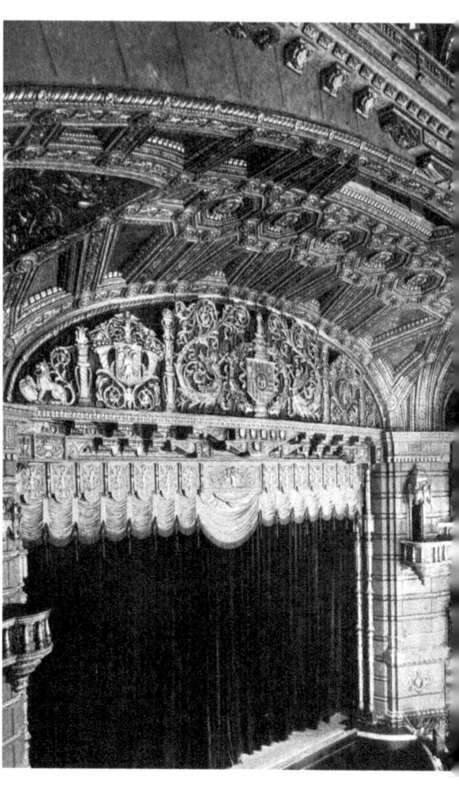

Above: Steep seating in the upper balcony of the Roxy Theatre, New York City.

Above right: Alschlager's Roxy Theatre stage is just for the screen.

The newly named Fox Oakland opened with the Fox Film Corporation movie *The Air Circus*. Besides the latest in sound technology, the Oakland theatre also had a Mighty Wurlitzer organ and the latest Westinghouse lamps and colored spotlights with the most recently developed switches. Originally blue draperies and colorful tapestries hung on the walls. Golden lighting fixtures impressed with colored jewels hung against a rich Islamic-patterned ceiling inlaid with mirrors which sparkled onto Hindu-inspired figures adorned with "emeralds" and "ruby" jewels lit from behind, while wisps of steam rose from golden urns in their hands. No oriental reference and illusion was missed. The Fox Oakland officially closed in 1966. After almost being torn down, it became an Oakland City Landmark in 1978, and was listed on the National Register of Historic Places in 1979.

The Fox Theatre, located at 527 North Grand Boulevard in St. Louis, Missouri, was one of five showcase theatres built by William Fox and was known as "The Fabulous Fox" when it opened on January 31, 1929. It was designed by Detroit-born Charles Howard Crane, and with 5,060 seats and a Mighty Wurlitzer, it was reported to be the second-largest theatre in the United States. Only the Roxy, in New York, popularly called "The Cathedral of the Motion Picture," had more seating—6,200 in 1927. A 1929 St. Louis newspaper reported on the Fox Theatre:

> Burmese shrine doors separate the lobby from the auditorium. Entering, one looks from between great Oriental arches ... to the great auditorium, its immense stage, deep-cushioned seats... The ceiling is swathed in Indian fabrics draped circularly from the center to the sides, while the canopied dome of the theatre is studded with brilliant stones... In the center hangs a giant chandelier, a globe 12 feet in diameter and 42 feet in circumference ... tassel fringe and filigree embellish the canopied ceiling which is supported by giant spears.
>
> Atmospheric cloud effects play upon the hangings, changing their colors with the mood of the music and the various program features.

Visually dazzling in its bewildering décor William Fox called it the "Eve Leo Style" after his wife, who contributed to the design, whom he had married in 1899, when he was twenty and she sixteen. The interiors were conflations of their travels and her dreams—time and place wrapped into one, just like

Towering columns of red scagliola in the Detroit Fox's foyer.

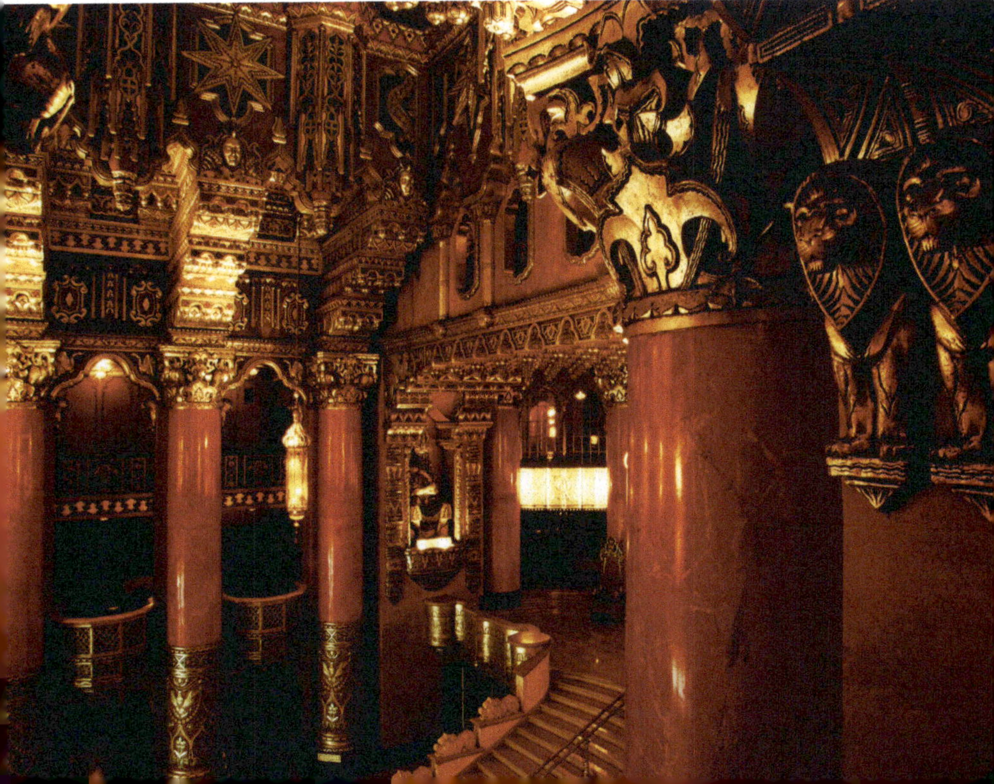

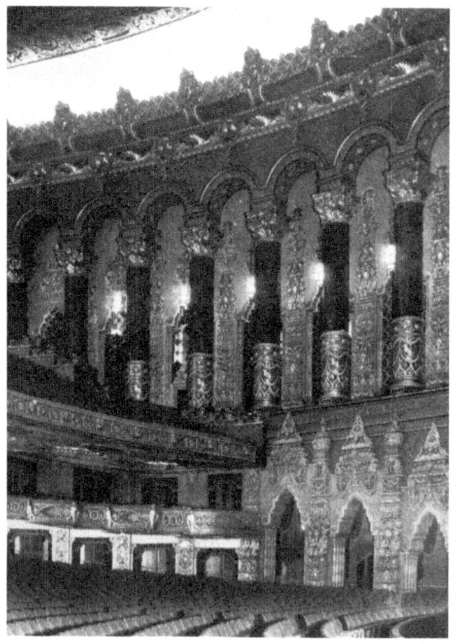

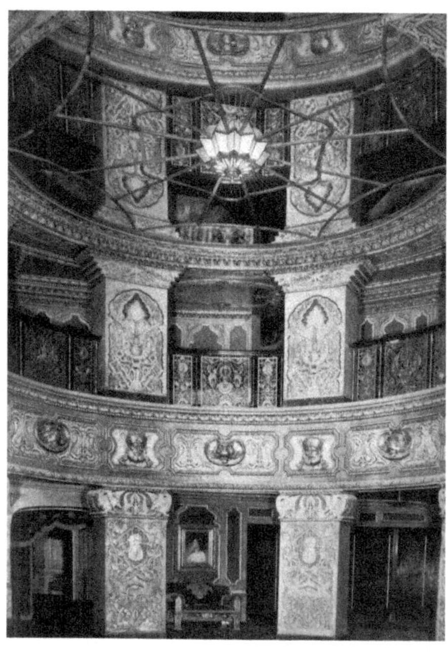

Above: A Byzantine fantasy world lines the auditorium of the Detroit Fox.

Above right: The Fox's foyer in Detroit starts the oriental faux fantasy in this theatre.

in film. The St. Louis Fox has its twin in the Detroit Fox, which opened a year earlier at 2211 Woodward Avenue, Detroit, designed by the same architect.

Laurie J. Marzejka of *The Detroit News* reported that when the opening-night curtain rose at Detroit's Fox Theatre on September 21, 1928, an audience of five thousand invited guests came to marvel at what was being billed as a "Temple of Amusement," a genie's world of Far Eastern, Indian

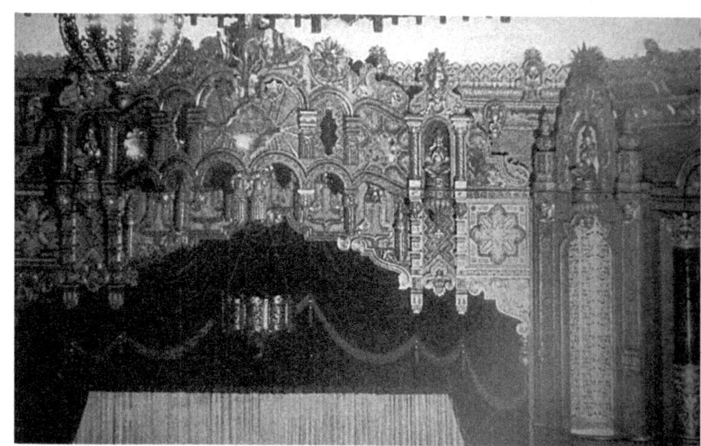

Detroit meets oriental fantasy atop the Fox stage.

and Egyptian styles, all in one room. They did not go home disappointed.

Though both the St. Louis and the Detroit interiors were designed by Eve Leo, the Fox in Detroit was said to be grander than its twin and even surpassed the Roxy in the opinion of many who knew both, or all three. Designed by architect C. Howard Crane who had once worked for Albert Kahn, the exterior of the lobby of the Detroit Fox stood a mammoth ten stories. Each blood-red scagliola column was topped by a jeweled figure representing an Asian deity now lost to the vapors of history. Exotically modest golden damask draperies combined with regal-red velour embraced by festoons with wide silken fringes lined the walls like so many stage hands, while over the entrance a small Moller organ rained notes over the guests who stood on a wool rug weighing 3,000 pounds in a 3,600-square-foot lobby. No luxury was enough for Eve Leo at the Fox.

UNITED ARTISTS

Despite the luxury of theatres like the Detroit Fox, the realities of the movie industry were harsh. Actors were on the screen and adored by the public, yet the movie's financiers, producers and directors pulled the strings that brought life to the actors. In 1919, four actors/directors, D. W. Griffith, Charlie Chaplin, Mary Pickford, Douglas Fairbanks, and a lawyer, William Gibbs McAdoo, formed a joint venture they named United Artists. The idea was to give actors more say and power in the movie-making process. At first they produced films, but quickly evolved, like their competition, into owning theatres, too. In Chicago they acquired the Apollo Theatre in 1927. The Apollo, 45 West Randolph Street, was built in 1921 at the corner of Randolph and Dearborn for A. H. Woods after designs by Holabird and Roche. United Artists commissioned C. Howard Crane to remodel it into a Spanish Moorish dream, akin to the Los Angeles United Artists Theatre, but smaller, seating only 1,703 and lacking a stage. With its colorful scagliola walls and columns and painted tiles, the lobby felt Moorish/Ottoman; its auditorium ceiling was a giant cove-lit dome encircled by ten small oculi. Retaining its name, four years later Balaban & Katz took over the operations of the theatre and it continued as a movie palace into the 1970s. In 1991 it was razed.

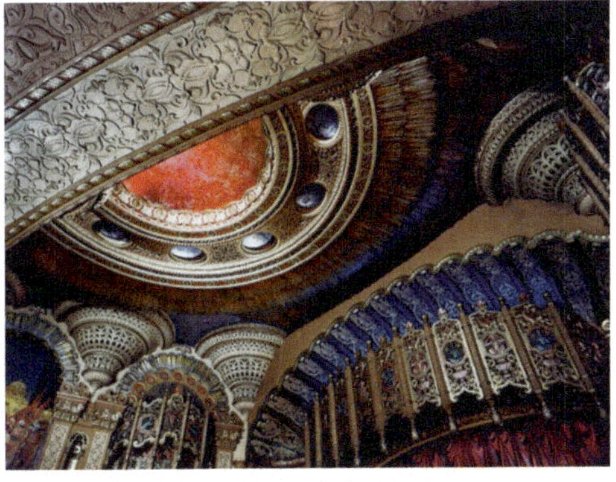

Once upon a time there was color and form in Chicago's United Artists Theatre.

The United Artists Theatre, at 140 Bagley Avenue in Detroit, was opened on February 3, 1928, and significantly contributed to the increasing number of theaters around Grand Circus Park's unique radial street plan. As with other theatres of the time, it was housed within an office building, both designed by C. Howard Crane. Not quite as ornate as its Los Angeles namesake, the building rose eighteen stories. It was faced in orange brick over a two-story stone base distinguished by a two-story arcade of windows and entrance ways. The top was lined with a row of round-headed windows. Overall, it was designed in the conventional scheme of a skyscraper topped with a decorative cornice. Two entrances led into the building. The right one, marked by a broad canopy marquee and a seven-story vertical sign, led to the theatre's lobby.

The Detroit United Artists auditorium, seating 2,070, displayed the same heavy drippings of Spanish Gothic decoration as the LA United Artists. Both featured a gilded dome, lace-like fan vaults and massive ornamental canopies over the proscenium and organ screens. The only features that distinguished the Detroit auditorium from its

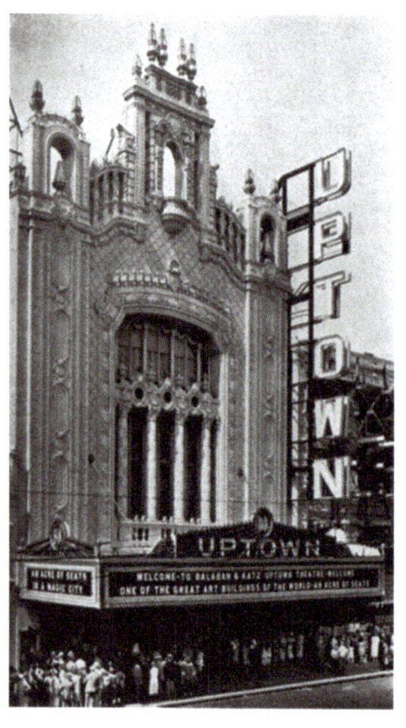

Once a neighborhood giant, Chicago's Uptown Theatre.

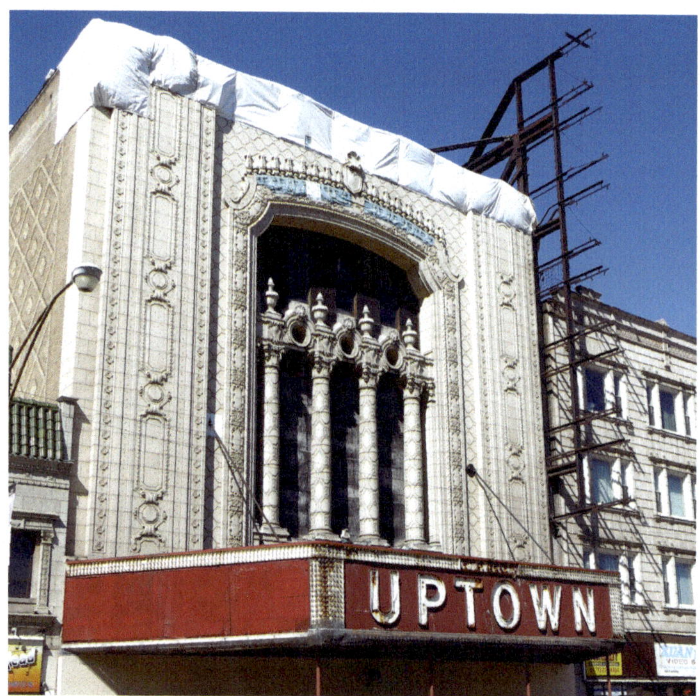

Since 2006, Chicago's Uptown Theatre upper façade has been in storage, resulting in a fair shadow of its former greatness.

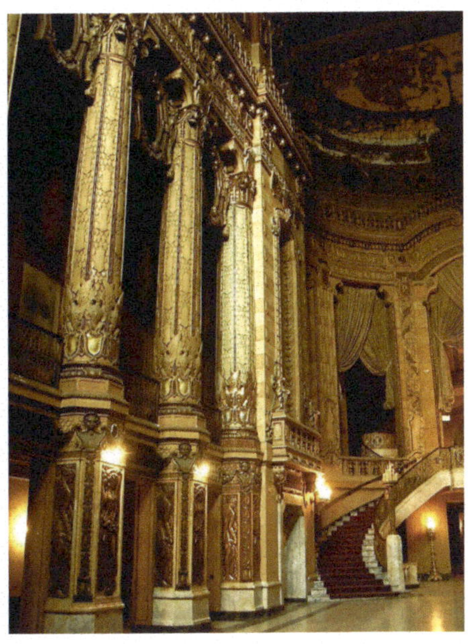

Above left: Plaster retains some of its former glory in the foyer of Chicago's Uptown Theatre.

Above: One of the many enormous plaster capitals of the Uptown Theatre.

Los Angeles predecessor were "a few Indian maidens," and a lessening of the stalactite clustering. The overall appearance of the two auditoria was quite similar; Crane even reused the plaster molds from Los Angeles to create the interior ornament for Detroit. Both Crane and Thomas Lamb proved most successfully that they had "learned the economy of duplication." The studios responded favorably to this practice, since it gave their theatre chains a distinctive and memorable stylistic identity, as well as trimming building expenses.

In 1928, while Lamb was designing a series of Loew's theatres characterized by a "Mexican Baroque" style, Crane continued in full force with the United Artists' "Spanish Gothic" theme.

SPANISH BAROQUE IS EASY IN TERRACOTTA

"An Acre of seats in a Magic City," the Uptown Theatre designed by Rapp & Rapp, built by Balaban & Katz at 4816 North Broadway in Chicago in Spanish Baroque-, Mission- and Tudor-inspired styles, opened August 18, 1925. With 4,381 seats, the auditorium is said to be larger than that of any other movie palace in the United States. It stood on 46,000 square feet of land. At its opening, a "Central Uptown Parade" of over two hundred floats, and a grand ball introduced the "Magic City" and more than twelve thousand people stood in line to buy tickets for the first show. Several fainted. Inside, a staff of more than 130—including a full-time thirty-four-

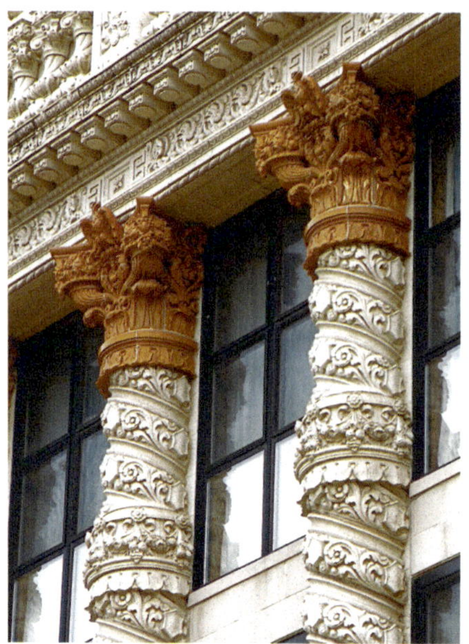

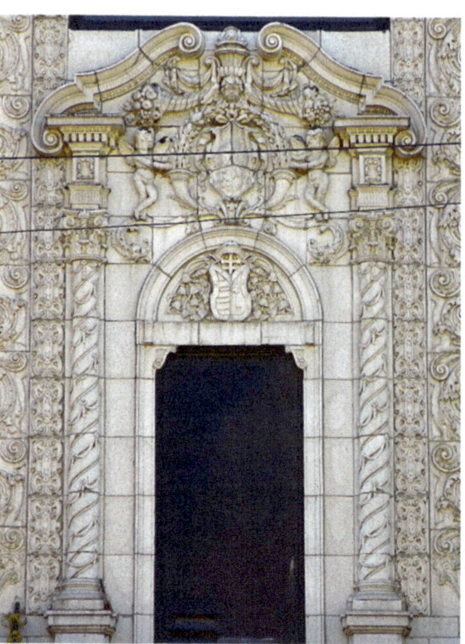

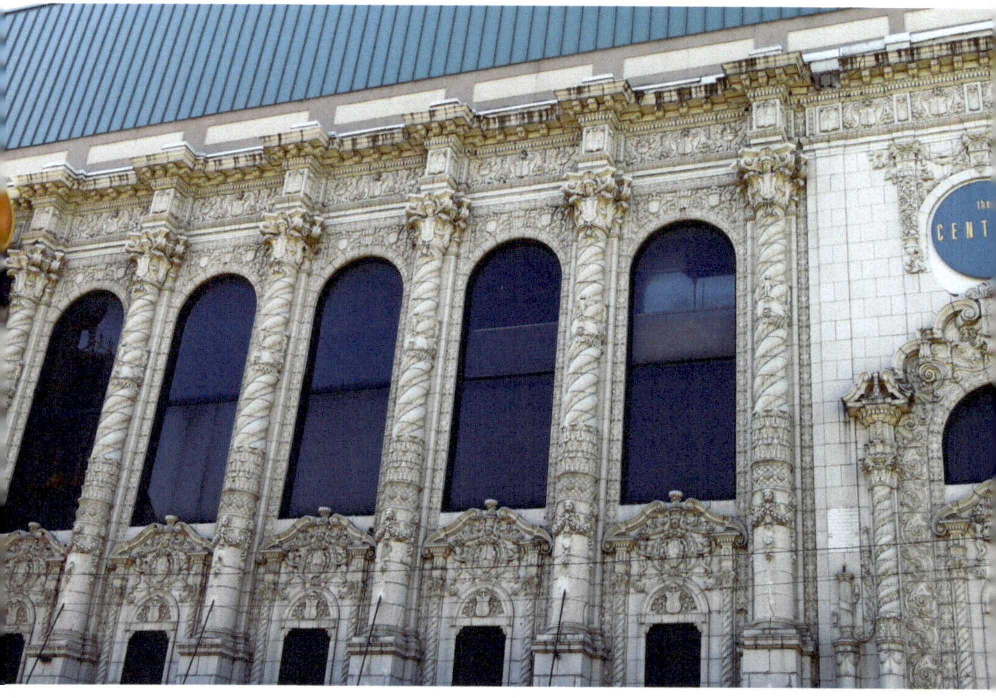

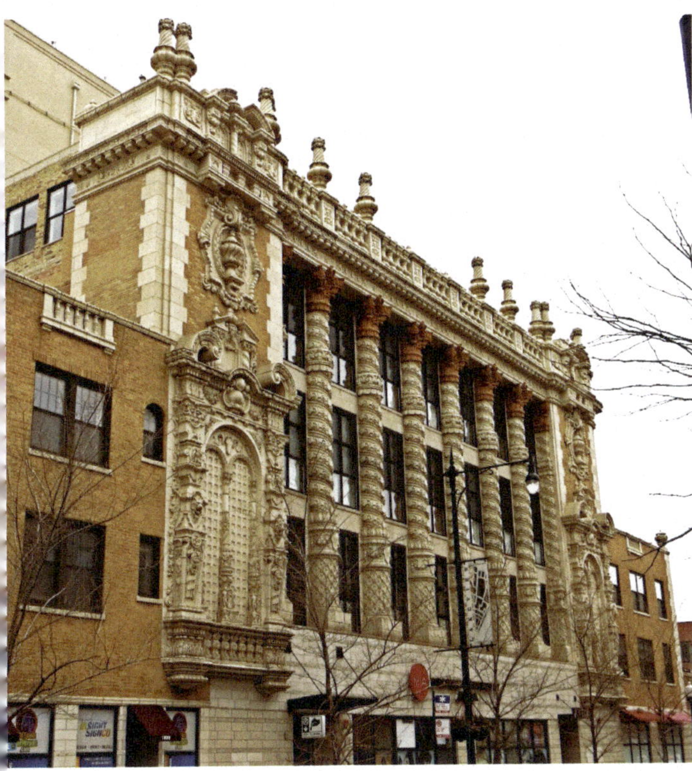

Left: Chicago had several Solomonic facades. This is the Belmont Theatre (1925), designed by Walter W. Ahlschlager.

Opposite, top left: The complexities of Spanish Baroque sculpture were copied in terracotta at the Belmont.

Opposite, top right: Terracotta doesn't get more complex than in this extravaganza designed by Edward Eichenbaum.

Opposite, bottom: Six Solomonic faux Spanish Baroque terracotta columns create a giant façade with acute cenophobia on Chicago's former Diversey Theatre.

piece orchestra, a nurse, and firemen—awaited the crowd. Each show had its own stage show production that followed the theme of the movie shown. This was more than vaudeville.

Constructed at 2828 N. Clark for the Orpheum circuit in Chicago, and opening on July 30, 1925, the Diversey retains only its Spanish Baroque-inspired terracotta façade designed by Edward C. Eichenbaum (1897–1982) of Levy & Klein architects, Chicago. A colonnade of giant creamy-white terracotta twisted Solomonic-styled columns looms over the street. Though ancient, the twisted "S"-curve shaft as seen here is a feature of Catholic Baroque architecture, especially Spanish Baroque, and is inspired by Bernini's use of them in the Baldacchino inside St. Peter's Basilica, Rome.

Another row of terracotta Solomonic Spanish Baroque giants make up the façade of the former 3,257-seat Belmont Theatre, 1632 W. Belmont Avenue, Chicago. It also opened in 1925, as a jewel of the Lubliner & Trinz circuit. Designed by Walter W. Ahlschlager—of Roxy in New York City fame—it was the entertainment heart of the neighborhood retail district known then as Lincoln-Belmont. By the end of the decade the Orpheum

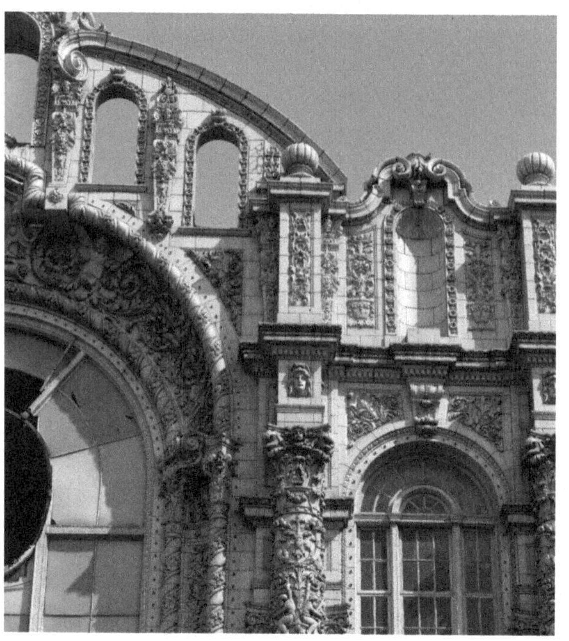

circuit briefly claimed the Belmont before Balaban & Katz took over in 1930. Today only the façade, rendered in white and gold glazed terracotta, remains.

The Granada Theatre, a 3,422-seat Spanish Baroque pile at 6427–41 North Sheridan Road in Chicago, was built in 1926 as the standard-bearer of the Marks Brothers theatre empire in the midwest, by Edward C. Eichenbaum of Levy & Klein. Though from New York, the Marks Brothers were major movie palace builders and operators in Chicago in 1925 through the mid-1930s, trying to parry every Balaban & Katz pivot with every theatre they constructed or managed.

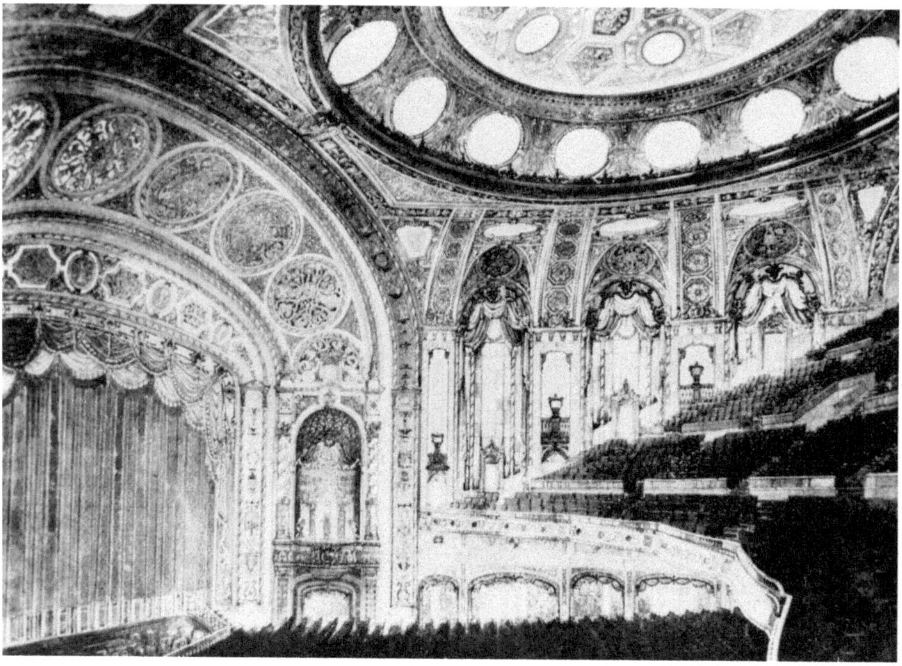

The Granada is acclaimed as Eichenbaum's finest design. The architects, Alexander L. Levy (1872–1955) and William J. Klein, the engineer of the firm (died in 1970), worked on several theatres in Chicago. Edward Eichenbaum, had apprenticed with Albert Kahn in Detroit before joining Levy & Klein in 1924. To get the right "look" for this 92-foot high Spanish Baroque inspiration, inside and out, Eichenbaum said he took actual Renaissance and Baroque decorative motifs from palaces, churches and villas in Italy and Spain saying, "if there was a crack in the marble of the original, then we kept it or put it in the plaster reproduction." The Granada was the most authentic of Chicago's Spanish Baroque movie palaces. It was willfully destroyed in 1990.

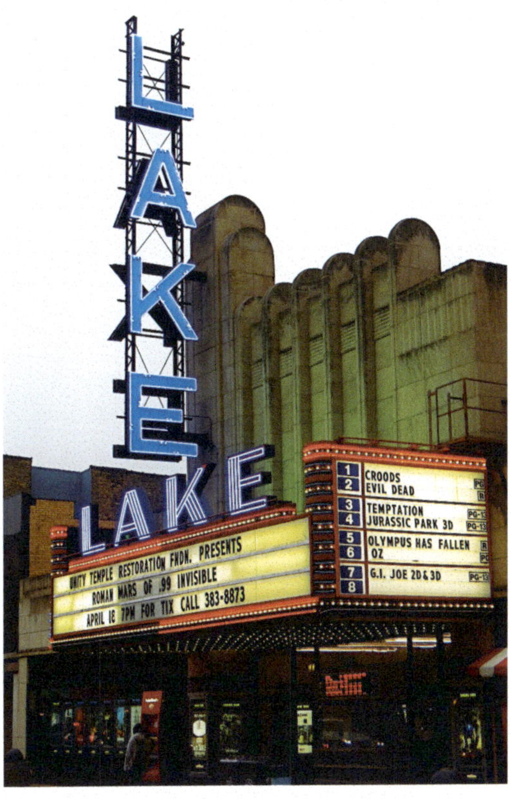

However, through salvage efforts, this and other movie palaces have not died or vanished from memory. Much of its terracotta façade and interior elements were salvaged and sold, and now decorate homes and gardens in Chicago and across the midwest, while a large crystal chandelier hangs in the Riviera, a smaller theatre in the Music Box on Southport.

Besides marking its spot with a giant façade, each movie palace also played with a giant sign of "liquid fire," as many described neon's cutting luminescence. Neon had been discovered in 1898 and its bright red glow, confined in Geissler tubes, became a popular sensation. Taking the natural next step beyond the Geissler tubes and Daniel McFarlan Moore's invention of a nitrogen-based light, French chemist and inventor Georges Claude (1870–1960) produced brilliant red neon tube lighting as a byproduct of his air liquefaction business. Claude demonstrated neon at the Paris Motor Show in December 1910 and five years later he secured a US patent. The US patent gave his company, Claude Neon Lights, a monopoly through the early 1930s. Los Angeles saw liquid fire first when, in 1923, Earle C. Anthony spent $2,500 on two signs with neon tubing spelling "Packard" for his Los Angeles Packard dealership. Movie palace marquees were not far behind.

Above: Oak Park's Lake Theatre neon marquee letters have been in place since 1936.

Opposite, top: Chicago, Granada Theatre. Spanish Baroque terracotta.

Opposite, bottom: Chicago, Granada Theatre. This was the most detailed Spanish Baroque interior in Chicago.

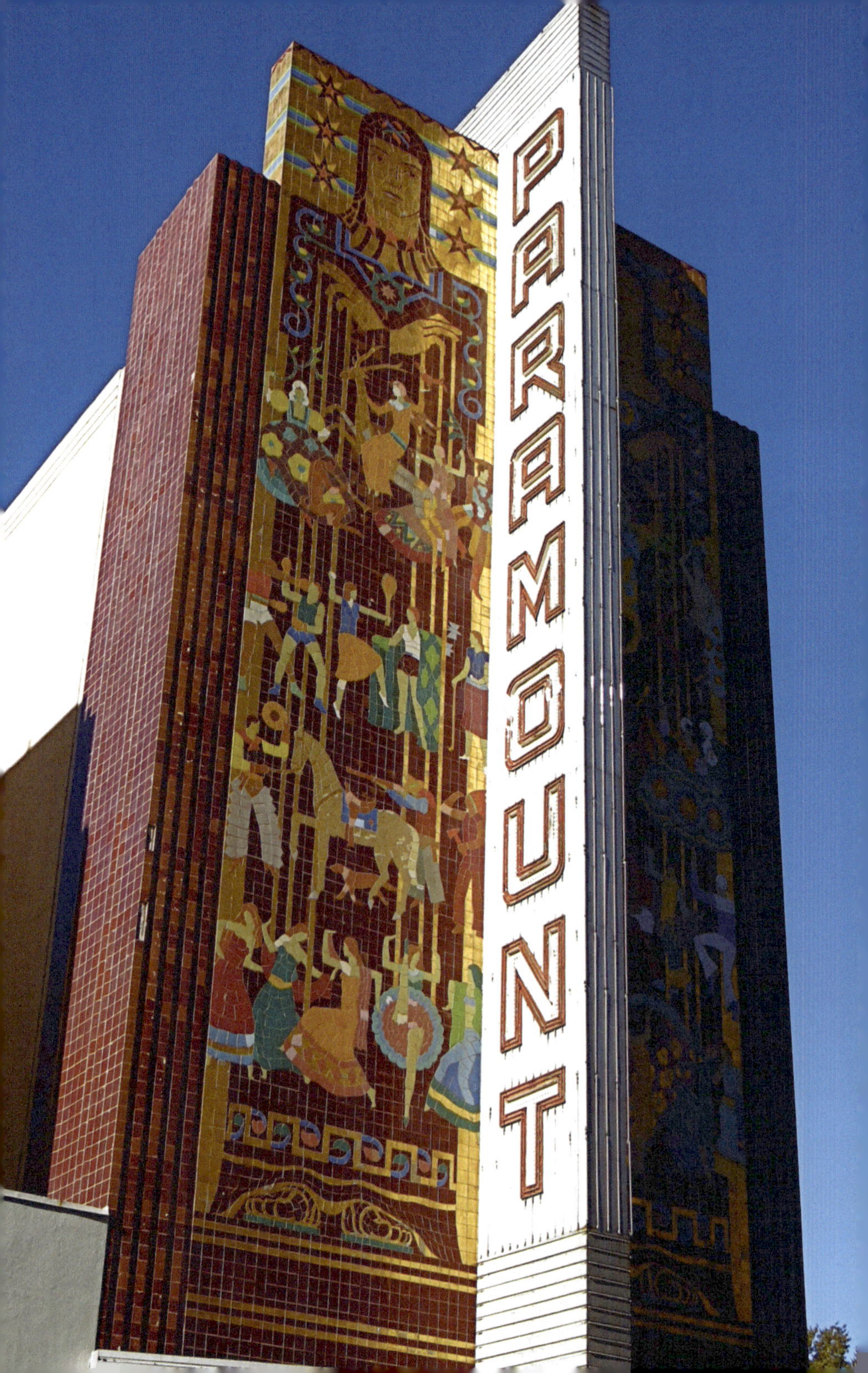
PARAMOUNT

OUT WITH FANTASY, IN WITH RATIONAL MODERN

When Adolph Zukor's Paramount Publix opened the Paramount on December 16, 1931, it was the largest multi-purpose movie palace on the west coast, seating 3,476. Its marquee was 110 feet tall, with enormous tile mosaic figures. Designed by thirty-eight-year-old Timothy L. Pflueger of Miller and Pflueger, it ushered in a new era in theatre design—Deco. Not only in Oakland was there a change in what was expected in a theatre; it swept across the United States on the wings of the Depression.

The marquee had two oversized red drapes of tile teeming with figures and animals, one on each side of the neon sign proclaiming it the Paramount. The Paramount's 58-foot-high grand lobby, with side walls of alternating vertical bands of warm green artificial light panels and muted red piers, and with both ends and ceiling decorated with an almost luminescent grillwork, was a superb example of Pflueger's lighting skill.

Attending the premier on December 5, 1931, was Kay Francis, star of the film *The False Madonna*, and cast members including William Boyd—soon to be a box-office favorite known as Hopalong Cassidy—mingled with California's governor, James Rolph, and Oakland mayor Fred N. Morcom. Tickets were first-come, first-served: 60 cents for the balcony seats and 85 cents for a seat in the orchestra. The house was packed.

Setting the pace for the look of the era to come, rare and costly materials were everywhere: hand-adzed quarter-sawn oak, Hungarian ash crotch, bird's-eye maple, Balinese rosewood, Malaysian teak, and Italian marble pleased the eye at every blink. No slurry of Baroque or Renaissance patterns and tired materials from the past, the Paramount sported a new look from a positive, machine-driven future. Pflueger lavished his lighting skills on the auditorium, with its gilded galaxies of whorls, and gold walls with sculpted motifs from the Bible and mythology. Even the Paramount's organ was special: a four-manual, twenty-rank Wurlitzer called the Publix I (Opus 2164), which cost $20,000 in 1931! There was also a twenty-six-piece orchestra. This, and much more, cost $27,000 per week to maintain—it didn't last for long.

Opposite: Oakland, Paramount. The marquee is large and modern, ushering in an end to movie palaces.

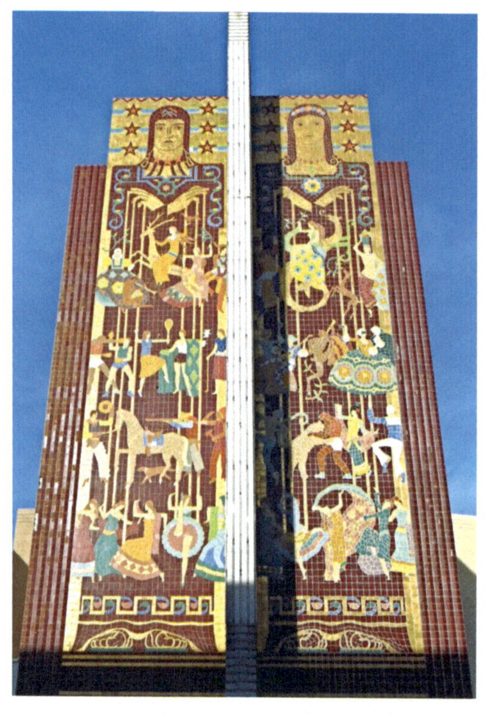

First came sound, then the Great Depression, and the exotic romanticism of escaping to the movie palace turned to the adulation of stars on the screen, not ceiling. Escape no longer came with popcorn in exotic locals, but in Milk Duds taming the hard-edged reality of everyday life through science and machines. Movie palaces became more than eye candy; they became the home of the spoken word, which demanded full attention and a clean wall for its waves to lap emotions across a seated crowd. References to hundreds of years of culture were purged from movie palaces by pragmatic colors, chrome, streamlined candy counters and giant neon marquees visible deep into the night to passing automobiles. Seemingly before dawn, machine and streamline Deco rendered the movie palace's misty whirl of exotic Beaux Arts fantasies, even along main street America, dusty, sentimental dreams.

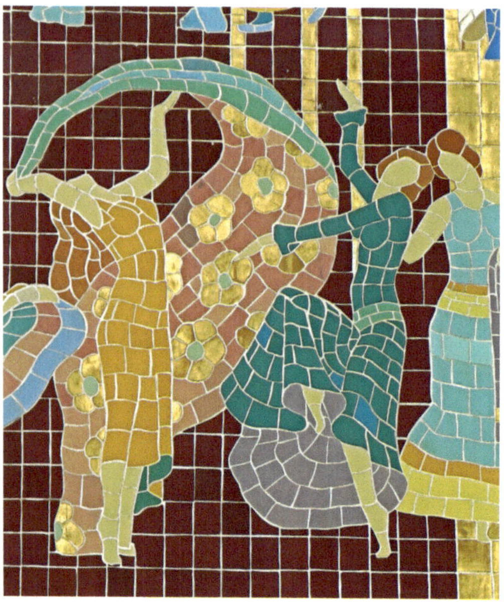

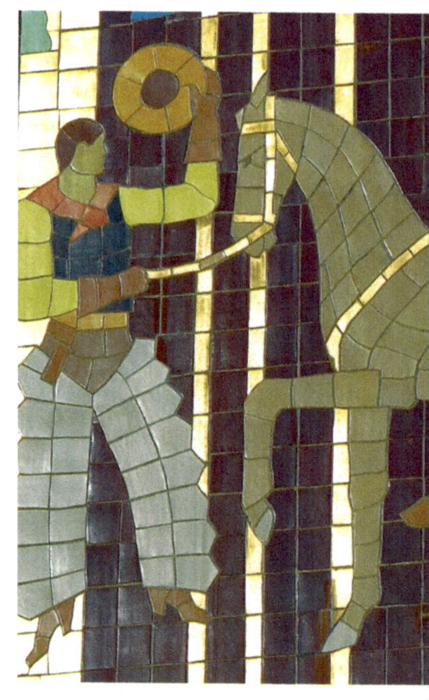

PLACES TO VISIT

In many American cities, movie palaces are a focal point of civic pride and are well marketed as such through historic theatre foundations.

Theatre Historical Society of America, York Theatre Building, 152 N. York Street, 2nd floor, Elmhurst, Illinois 60126-2806. Tel: (630) 782-1800. Website: www.historictheatres.org/
The society is a national resource for all topics related to theatres. Its museum exhibits regularly change, showcasing selections from its collections, and its archives hold information on more than 17,000 theatres and cover every period and style of theatre architecture.

Opposite top: Representing the now and not a distant past, male and female "gods" pull the strings of action in the façade mural of the Oakland Paramount.

Opposite bottom left and right: Modern dancers twirl across the Oakland's façade of dancers, while "movie" cowboys train horses.

Most large city movie palaces are found clustered along a street or intersection of several streets. In Chicago the traditional movie palaces were along Randolph Street or immediately north and south on cross streets—State, Dearborn, Clark. There are also theatres, some, as mentioned in the text, grand, others cozy, in each of the city's neighborhoods. In New York they are scattered across Manhattan, but tightly clustered around Times Square, Broadway and then in each of the city's boroughs. Los Angeles and Hollywood, understandably, both have a wealth of movie palaces strung along Broadway and then again on Hollywood Boulevard. In St. Louis the Fabulous Fox is like an island on North Grand Boulevard, away from the downtown. A similar concept exists in Detroit, where the Fox is in an office building on Woodward, while others are gathered around Grand Circus Park and Bagley Avenue.

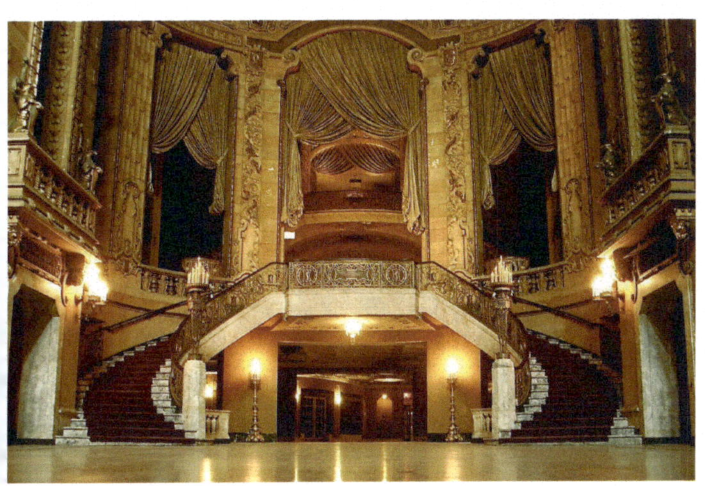

In the Uptown Theatre, Chicago, the grand stairs remain grand.

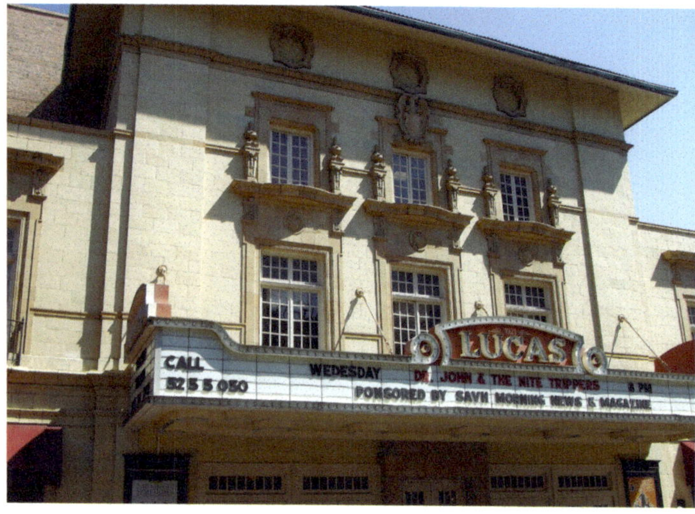

Opening in 1921, Arthur Lucas and architect C. K. Howell took more than two years to design the Lucas Theatre with Renaissance Revival and Adamesque details.

The San Francisco Neighborhood Theater Foundation has worked hard to landmark local movie palaces. The Metro at 2055 Union Street was declared a landmark in 2009 and is slowly being refurbished. The Richmond District's Alexandria Theatre remains closed with active redevelopment plans. The Castro Theatre remains vital. At 1192 Market Street, corner of Hyde, San Francisco's Orpheum Theatre remains intact and continues to wow audiences, as does the Golden Gate in the Tenderloin, at 1 Taylor Street. Across the Bay in Oakland, the Parkway Theatre, on Park Avenue closed in 2009, but is still there and may reopen. With the help of the Friends of the Cerrito Theatre it survives with its wonderful murals. There are plans for Oakland's Fox to reopen as a live music venue. Nearby, the Paramount has been carefully restored and its magnificent murals by Anthony B. Heinsbergen can be seen and the Mighty Wurlitzer heard when vintage movies in 35mm prints are shown or during tours on the first and third Saturday of each month.

Beale Street in Memphis, know for blues and jazz, was a movie palace hub, too. Today only a few movie palaces remain. The Daisy at 329 Beale welcomes with a grand half-dome entrance. It is now mostly used as a banquet hall. The Orpheum, 203 S. Main at Beale Street, is a now a stop for Broadway shows and sometimes its Mighty Wurlitzer can be heard. The Majestic at 145 S. Main Street has been converted into the Majestic Grill, a fine restaurant that shows silent films and classic movies on its private screen. Arguably Memphis' most famous theatre is the Memphian at 51 S. Cooper. Rented in the 1960s by Elvis Presley to watch films with his friends, the Theatre closed in 1985 and reopened a year later as the Playhouse on the Square.

FURTHER READING

Balaban, David. Foreword by Joseph R. DuciBella. *The Chicago Movie Palaces of Balaban and Katz*. Arcadia Publishing, Chicago, 2006.

DiChiera, Lisa. *The Theater Designs of C. Howard Crane*. MA Thesis, University of Pennsylvania, 1992.

Hall, Ben M. *The Best Remaining Seats: The Golden Age of the Movie Palace*. Da Capo Press, Cambridge, 1988.

Junchen, David L. *The Wurlitzer Pipe Organ: An Illustrated History*. The American Theatre Organ Society, 2005.

Melnick, Ross and Fuchs, Andreas. *Cinema Treasures: A New Look at Classic Movie Theaters*. Motorbooks International, Osceola, Wisconsin, 2004.

Sexton, R. W. and Betts, B. F. *American Theatres To-day*. vol. 1, Architecture Book Club, New York, 1927, vol. 2, 1930. Reprinted by Theatre Historical Society of America, Elmhurst, 2009.

Valentine, Maggie. *The Show Starts on the Sidewalk: An Architectural History of the Movie Theatre, Starring S. Charles Lee*. Yale University Press, New Haven, 1996.

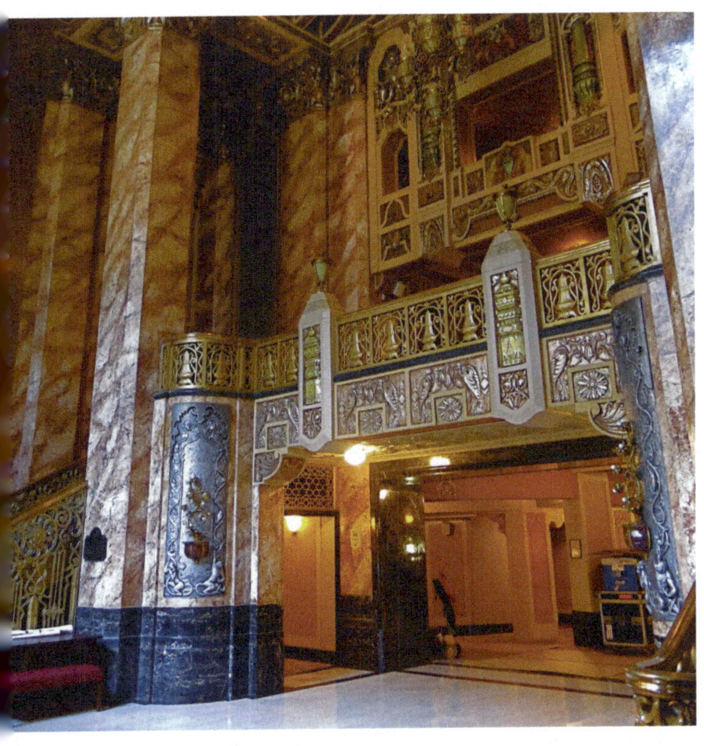

There is no marble at the Oriental in Chicago, only plaster.

INDEX

Page numbers in italics refer to illustrations

Printed and bound by CPI Group (UK) Ltd, Croydon, CR0 4YY

06/07/2026

02158986-0011